THIS PAGE INTENTIONALLY LEFT BLANK

THIS PAGE INTENTIONALLY LEFT BLANK

Giuseppe Verdi

Falstaff

OPERA STUDY GUIDE

AND

LIBRETTO

OPERA CLASSICS LIBRARY™SERIES

Edited by Burton D. Fisher
Principal lecturer, *Opera Journeys Lecture Series*

Opera Journeys™ Publishing   /   Boca Raton, Florida

WEBSITE: www.operajourneys.com   E MAIL: operaj@bellsouth.net

Contents

Opera Journeys™ Mini Guide Series

Opera Classics Library™ Series

Opera Journeys™ Libretto Series

A History of Opera:
Milestones and Metamorphoses

Mozart's Da Ponte Operas

PUCCINI COMPANION

Verdi Companion: 27 Opera Study Guide

Over 125 GUIDES & LIBRETTI AVAILABLE: Print or Ebook

•The Abduction from the Seraglio •Adriana Lecouvreur •L'Africaine •Aida
•Andrea Chénier •Anna Bolena •Ariadne auf Naxos •Armida •Attila
•The Ballad of Baby Doe •The Barber of Seville •Duke Bluebeard's Castle
•La Bohème •Boris Godunov •Candide •Capriccio •Carmen
•Cavalleria Rusticana •Cendrillon •La Cenerentola •La Clemenza di Tito
•Le Comte Ory •Così fan tutte •The Crucible •La Damnation de Faust
•The Death of Klinghoffer •Doctor Atomic •Don Carlo •Don Giovanni
•Don Pasquale •La Donna del Lago •The Elixir of Love •Elektra •Ernani
•Eugene Onegin •Exploring Wagner's Ring •Falstaff •La Fanciulla del West
•Faust •La Fille du Régiment •Fidelio •Die Fledermaus •The Flying Dutchman
•Die Frau ohne Schatten •Der Freischütz •Gianni Schicchi •La Gioconda
•Hamlet •Hansel and Gretel •Henry VIII •Iolanta •L'Italiana in Algeri
•Les Huguenots •Iphigénie en Tauride •Julius Caesar •Lakmé •Lohengrin
•Lucia di Lammermoor •Macbeth •Madama Butterfly •The Magic Flute
•The Makropolis Case •Manon •Manon Lescaut •Maria Stuarda
•The Marriage of Figaro •A Masked Ball •Die Meistersinger •The Mikado
•Nabucco •Nixon in China •Norma •Of Mice and Men •Orfeo ed Euridice
•Otello •I Pagliacci •Parsifal •The Pearl Fishers •Pelléas et Mélisande
•Porgy and Bess •Prince Igor •I Puritani •The Queen of Spades
•The Rake's Progress •The Rape of Lucretia •The Rhinegold •Rigoletto
•The Ring of the Nibelung •Roberto Devereaux •Rodalinda •Roméo et Juliette
•La Rondine •Der Rosenkavalier •Rusalka •Salome •Samson and Delilah
•Show Boat •Siegfried •Simon Boccanegra •La Sonnambula •Suor Angelica
•Susannah •Il Tabarro •The Tales of Hoffmann •Tannhäuser •Thaïs •Tosca
•La Traviata •Tristan and Isolde •Il Trittico •Les Troyens •Il Trovatore
•Turandot •The Valkyrie •Werther •West Side Story •Wozzeck

WWW.OPERAJOURNEYS.COM

a *Prelude*........

OPERA CLASSICS LIBRARY's
Falstaff
STUDY GUIDE WITH LIBRETTO

After Verdi completed the final act of *Falstaff*, he accompanied it with a note to Ricordi, his publisher, paraphrasing a passage in Boito's libretto:

"It is all finished. Go, go, old John. Go on your way for as long as you can. Amusing rogue, forever true beneath the masks you wear in different times and places. Go, go, on your way. Farewell."

Falstaff possesses timeless humor and gaiety. In certain respects, it captures the golden warmth and ironic laughter of Verdi's old age — it remains a testament to Verdi, as well as a magnificent comic farewell from the master of music drama.

OPERA CLASSICS LIBRARY explores the greatness of Wagner's *Lohengrin*. The *Commentary and Analysis* deals with the opera's genesis, biographical and chronological elements and its premiere and performance history.

The text also contains a *Brief Story Synopsis, Principal Characters* in *Lohengrin,* and a *Story Narrative with Music Highlight Examples,* the latter containing original music transcriptions that are interspersed within the story's dramatic exposition. In addition, the text includes a *Dictionary of Opera and Musical Terms.*

The *Libretto* provides the translation in a side-by-side format and includes *Music Highlight Examples.*

The opera art form is the sum of many artistic expressions: theatrical drama, music, scenery, poetry, dance, acting and gesture. In opera, the music composer who is the dramatist; he applies the emotive power of his music and the kinetic intensity of the prose to provide powerful theater, an impact on one's sensibilities that can reach into the very depths of the human soul.

Burton D. Fisher
Editor
OPERA CLASSICS LIBRARY

Falstaff

Opera in Italian opera in three acts

**Music
by
Giuseppe Verdi**

**Libretto by Arrigo Boito
after Shakespeare's
The Merry Wives of Windsor (1600)
Henry IV, Part One (1597)
Henry IV, Part Two (1598)**

**Premiere: Teatro alla Scala, Milan,
February, 1893**

Commentary and Analysis

Giuseppe Verdi was a man possessing formidable artistic and human integrity. He dissolved his whole self into his art. He was a man of profound compassion: a moralist and humanitarian sensitive to the injustices in the world; at times, he considered himself a priest dedicated through his art to awaken man to morality and humanity.

Temperamentally, Verdi was a child of Enlightenment ideals: he possessed a noble conception of humanity that abominated absolutism and deified civil liberty. He struggled against tyranny in all its forms during his entire lifetime: personal, social, political, or ecclesiastical. Verdi would use the opera art form to convey his sense of profound human idealism: opera enabled him to achieve his goals by combining the potency of text with the emotive power of music.

Early in his career, Verdi had become a national hero of his beloved Italy: his operas provided the musical inspiration for his country's struggle for unity and independence. IN the 16 operas he composed from 1839 to 1851, each opera contained underlying nationalistic themes that glorified liberty and freedom. Symbolically and allegorically, Verdi's oeuvre portrayed the Italian people suffering under the oppression of foreign countries: Austria, France, and even the Papacy. His music would be imbedded with patriotic aspirations, and became the anthems for Italian liberation. Even the letters of his name was envisioned as an anagram for Italy's nationalistic aspirations: V E R D I represented *Vittorio Emanuelo Re d'Italia,* a call for the return of the exiled King Victor Emanuel to rule Italy. The mourners at Verdi's funeral sang the inspirational "Va pensioro" chorus of the Hebrew exiles from *Nabucco* (1842), Verdi's third opera — a profound and impassioned tribute to an esteemed Italian patriot.

Verdi's early musical style mirrored the Italian "primo ottocento" — the early 19th century bel canto era that had become the trademark of his predecessors: Rossini, Bellini, and Donizetti. In the bel canto genre, vocal virtuosity dominated the art form, and dramatic effects were rendered through a singer's inflection and articulation: words and text were secondary to vocal art. Bel canto operas generally featured a series of arias and set-pieces, which provided the characters' reflections, self-revelation, and introspection, the pieces separated by recitative that would provide the action. In the traditions and conventions of 19th-century Italian opera, operas were not unified or integrated into an organic whole, either textually, musically, or dramatically — the ideal of music drama on the opera stage was yet to mature.

As the 1850s unfolded, Verdi entered a new phase in his career. The bel canto was in decline, and his burning mission for Italy's independence represented an imminent fait accompli. Verdi decided to abandon the heroic pathos and nationalistic themes of his early operas and seek more profound operatic subjects: bold subjects with greater dramatic and psychological depth that accented spiritual values, intimate humanity, and tender emotions. From this point forward, Verdi became ceaseless in his goal to create an expressiveness and acute delineation of the human soul that had never before been realized on the opera stage.

The first opera of Verdi's "middle period" was *Rigoletto* (1851); his last opera was *Falstaff* (1893), which demonstrated that his creative art had continued to develop and flower, and strive toward more intense dramatic expression — works possessing an exceptional lyricism, greater fusion between text and music, and a more profound characterization of humanity.

The second half of the nineteenth century witnessed profound transformations in operatic expression: Gounod's *Faust* (1859) and *Roméo et Juliet* (1867) introduced the sublime traditions of the French lyrique; Bizet's *Carmen* (1875) portrayed the fiery passions of verismé; and

Wagner reinvented opera traditions and conventions with music dramas — the first operas of *Der Ring das Nibelungen*, *Das Rheingold* (1854) and *Die Walküre* (1856), followed by *Tristan und Isolde* (1859), and *Die Meistersinger* (1867). Nevertheless, Verdi reigned supreme as the standard bearer and icon of Italian opera.

During Verdi's "middle period," he composed some of his best-loved works: *Rigoletto* (1851); *Il Trovatore* (1853); *La Traviata* (1853); *I Vespri Siciliani* (1855); *Simon Boccanegra* (1857); *Aroldo* (1857); *Un Ballo in Maschera* (1859); *La Forza del Destino* (1862); *Don Carlo* (1867); and *Aïda* (1871).

When *Aïda* premiered (1871), Verdi seemed to have created the crowning glory of his career: *Aïda* was a grand opera, a magnificent blend of spectacle, dramatic action, intense melodic invention, and the portrayal of profound human passion. After *Aïda*, Verdi composed the *Requiem* (1874), a tribute to his idol, Alessandro Manzoni, the renowned Italian poet, and author of the classic novel, *I Promessi Sposi.*

In 1874, at the age of 61, Verdi felt that the time had come for him to fade from the world music scene and fulfill his life-long dream to retire to his farm at Sant'Agata. He also sensed that he had fallen from favor: that he had become isolated from the transformations and changes that were affecting contemporary opera. The avant-garde and modernists had accused him of being distinctly old-fashioned, passé, and out of touch with the times; the pan-Europeans had espoused Wagner's ideas and conceptions of music-drama, and the "giovanni scuola," the blossoming "Young School" of Italian verismo composers had introduced a new sense of dramatic truth and realism to operatic subjects.

Verdi, the great composer who dominated Italian and international opera for much of the nineteenth century, sensed that his star had fallen. In the end, he became despondent, bitter, melancholy, and frustrated. More importantly, he became disillusioned that Italian opera was losing its unique esteem and sinking beneath a tide of new aesthetic ideas that he was powerless to stem, in particular, Wagnerism.

Wagner had become a thorn in Verdi's later musical life; their differing operatic approaches resulted in a clash of operatic titans. Whereas Verdi's style focused on action and melody, Wagner's style was introspective. His later music dramas were solidly "through composed" with their text and music integrated and enhanced through symphonic leitmotif development. The Wagnerian onslaught was so prevalent, that Giulio Ricordi, Verdi's powerful publisher, turned the city of Milan into a virtual stronghold of anti-Wagnerism.

Sixteen years after *Aïda*, in 1887, the seventy-four year-old composer was in retirement and relishing his golden years: it was the time when the fires of ambition were supposed to extinguish, and a time when most people become spectators in life rather than its stars. But despite his age, Verdi was lured out of self-imposed retirement and proceeded to astonish the musical world with his twenty-seventh opera, *Otello:* he demonstrated beyond all doubt that the fierce creative spirit that was burning within him was not only very much alive, but indeed a glorious living inspiration that still glowed brightly. Verdi's success with *Otello* epitomized the words of Robert Browning's Rabbi Ben Ezra: "Grow old along with me. The best is yet to be." Indeed, with *Otello,* Verdi overturned the equation and transformed his old age into a glory.

Otello was an Italian opera to the core and unequivocally challenged Verdi's contemporary critics. *Otello* became the Italian music of the future, a quintessential music drama composed in the Italian style that possessed the essential core of Italian opera: melody, lyricism, and vocal beauty. On the one hand, *Otello* represented a powerful demonstration of Verdi's incessant creative energy and capacity for self-renewal and continuing artistic maturity, but on the other hand, it single-handedly reestablished the supremacy and quality of the Italian operatic style.

The greatness of the opera art form is that it integrates words with music. Words provoke thought, but words combined with music, provoke feelings, emotions, and passions. Words sublimely fused with music can express what language alone has exhausted.

Verdi saturated *Otello* with a magnificent blend of melody together with swift dramatic action: his music endows the tragedy with melodramatic intensity and powerful human passion as the hero's sensibilities rapidly change as he heads towards the abyss of pathological destruction. Nevertheless, *Otello's* internal structural style retained past traditions: the opera indeed contains conventional arias, duets, and ensembles, but Verdi modernized them in terms of style and texture — a finite conception that provided a profound sense of musico-dramatic continuity.

In *Otello*, the structural unit of the *act* takes precedence over the *scene*, and as such, the opera contains an almost seamless stream of dramatic continuity. Librettist Boito's impassioned and powerful words fuse and integrate with Verdi's music score in an organic unity that endows the opera with an unrelenting pace, drive, and compulsion, all of which serve to emphasize emotion, passion, and more profound psychological confrontation.

Verdi sculpts confrontational situations with clear and vivid words that stand out in relief: his ideal of the "parola scenica" by which the particular word(s) overwhelm the situation and provide exceptional clarity. Quintessential examples, Amneris's "Trema vil schiava" ("Tremble vile slave") in *Aïda*, and *Otello*'s impassioned passionate explosion of vengeance, "Sangue, sangue, sangue!" ("Blood, blood, blood!").

Otello and *Falstaff*, Verdi's last operas, represent a logical evolution in the composer's development. These final masterpieces were written by a composer very different from the composer of *La Traviata, Il Trovatore, Don Carlo* or *Aida.*

With *Otello*, Verdi ordained the future of the Italian lyric theater: it became his own conception of Wagner's "gesamtkunstwerk," or "total artwork," certainly without artistic compromise to his genius or integrity. Verdi's heirs, Mascagni, Leoncavallo, Ponchielli, Cilea, Giordano, and Puccini, would continue the great tradition, most in the short-lived verismo genre. Nevertheless, all of their works would be saturated with a profound dramatic synthesis of words and music, all driven by profound melody and lyricism — the essence of the Italian opera style.

The evolution of *Otello*, and ultimately *Falstaff*, Verdi's final masterpiece, owes its provenance to Giulio Ricordi, Verdi's dynamic publisher, who foresaw the splendid possibilities of a flowering artistic partnership between the great composer and Arrigo Boito, the acclaimed poet. Nevertheless, creating that collaboration was a long and stormy operatic event in itself: Verdi and Boito were in the throes of a love-hate relationship that was saturated with intense passion. Verdi and Boito were incomparably diverse in terms of age, background, and temperament. Verdi came from humble peasant origins, and in personality and character, was extremely practical rather than philosophical. Boito was half-Polish, a man of letters, an opera composer, and a musician. But more importantly, he was one of those late nineteenth century pan-Europeans, who had idealized visions about the future of contemporary art.

Boito considered contemporary Italian opera in decay and degeneration: he launched an active crusade to modernize the art form and bring it painfully into the vanguard of modern European culture. He became associated with the "Scapigliatura" ("the Unkempt Ones"), a group of the avant-guard who were not only iconoclasts, but dedicated to ridding Italian art of all of its earlier traditions. Through satire and derision, the "scapigliati" ridiculed Italian opera. They envisioned its redemption in Wagner's "music of the future": it was the onset of the nineteenth century clash of opera titans, or Verdi vs. Wagner, or Italian opera vs. German music drama.

As a composer, Boito's seminal opera, *Mefistofele,* premiered at La Scala in 1868. Boito's music made no significant impression on Verdi, who considered its musical and dramatic integration too Wagnerian, the orchestration too heavy, and its use of leitmotifs rather amateurish. In particular, he felt that *Mefistofele* lacked essential musical development, and commented that he felt that its composer had renounced all form of melody for fear of losing touch with the text.

Contrarily, Boito was an antagonist who doubted if Verdi could continue to play a role in the future of Italian opera. Boito speculated about a new champion who would redeem Italian opera: "Perhaps the man is already born who will elevate the art of music in all its chaste purity above that altar now befouled like the walls of a brothel." Whether Boito's bombast was directed to Verdi or not, Verdi assumed that he was the specific target of Boito's vicious insults: the enemy of Italian art. As a result, Boito's presumed affront against Verdi remained an obstacle to Ricordi's efforts to unite the composer and poet, and their historical feud fed Verdi's mistrust and continued to undermine Ricordi's dream of their future collaboration.

Nevertheless, Verdi's personal reservations about Boito's ideals and musical talent precluded his respect and admiration for his literary talent. In 1862, in Paris, the twenty-year-old Boito, then a music student, had the honor of meeting both Rossini and Verdi. Verdi was impressed by Boito and commissioned him to write the text for the "Inno delle nazioni" ("The Hymn of the Nations"), a work that received prominence during World War II when Arturo Toscanini performed it copiously as a testament to allied opposition to Italian fascism.

As a librettist, Boito consistently believed that the key ingredient of music drama was to achieve fluidity between words and music: a continuous and swift succession of dramatic confrontations rather than patterns of reflection. As such, he strove to achieve greater realism and naturalism in a form of sung drama that approached rhythms and voice inflections, and that would be imitative of spoken theater.

Boito's primary strengths were his ability to simplify a complicated plot. He was a writer with a varied poetic language, a brilliant affinity for obscure polysyllables, and a keen sense of balance and proportion. Boito was the librettist for a number of all but forgotten operas, the single exception, his text written for Ponchielli's *La Gioconda* (1876), the opera's plot loosely derived from Hugo's *Angelo.* Boito changed the story's venue to Venice in order to introduce local color, however, it possessed a flamboyant melodramatic style that was bold and far from the subtle characterizations of Hugo.

Boito frequently wrote under the pseudonym *Tobio Gorrio,* an anagram of his name. Of his many literary achievements, he was instrumental in introducing German works to Italy, translating German lieder into Italian, among them Wagner's *Wesendonk Lieder,* as well as an Italian translation of Wagner's *Rienzi.*

Giulio Ricordi, now in the role of peacemaker, wisely understood a poet's ability to aid and stimulate the thoughts of a composer. In effect, Ricordi resolved to create a Verdi-Boito partnership similar to other classic composer-librettist collaborations: Lorenzo da Ponte with Mozart, and Hugo von Hofmannsthal with Richard Strauss. Ricordi astutely recognized that before Verdi and Boito could proceed toward the infinitely great task of *Otello,* they needed a "trial balloon," an opportunity to work together and test the chemistry of their relationship.

Ricordi initiated a series of intrigues that were coupled with diplomacy and tact. Boito had been working on his own opera, *Nerone,* and Ricordi learned that Verdi also had expressed interest in that same subject for a new opera. Ricordi persuaded Boito to magnanimously offer to relinquish the libretto to Verdi, but Verdi was still smoldering from Boito's earlier assault against Italian art, and Ricordi's attempt to create a Verdi-Boito collaboration on *Nerone* never materialized.

A more likely opportunity for a "trial balloon" was floating on the horizon. Verdi had been unhappy with the final libretto of *Simon Boccanegra* (1857), and he agreed to test Boito's talent by urging him to submit revisions. The results were immensely satisfying to Verdi: Boito added the Council Chamber scene to *Simon Boccanegra:* Verdi was ecstatic with the results and concluded that Boito had redeemed his opera.

Poet and composer became cautiously reconciled, and the door was now open for their possible collaboration on *Otello.* Verdi showed cautious enthusiasm for the project, hesitant to affront the venerated Rossini who had also composed *Otello* (1816). Nevertheless, after Boito submitted his libretto for *Otello* to Verdi, its dramatic qualities severely impressed him and sealed his collaboration with Verdi, a friendship and relationship Boito eventually regarded as the climax of his artistic life.

Verdi had a life-long veneration for Shakespeare, his singular and most popular source of inspiration; it was far more profound than the playwrights Goldoni, Goethe, Schiller, Hugo, and Racine. Verdi said of Shakespeare: "He is a favorite poet of mine whom I have had in my hands from earliest youth and whom I read and reread constantly."

Shakespeare's tragedies and comedies are well-suited to the opera medium: their themes are heavily saturated and dominated by extravagant passions involving love, hate, jealousy, and revenge. Yet transforming Shakespeare's theatrical art and poetic language into opera is intrinsically challenging because his works depend on lightning verbal intricacies, word-play, wit, and eloquent speech — an art driven by powerful words, and perhaps the reason that the scenarios of many operatic adaptations are far removed from the original subject.

Nevertheless, three of Verdi's operas have assured Shakespeare a place in Verdi's operatic canon: *Macbeth, Otello,* and *Falstaff.* Throughout Verdi's entire career, he contemplated bringing *Hamlet* and *King Lear* to the operatic stage: both projects represented ambitions that never reached fruition. In later life, Boito submitted a sketch to Verdi for *King Lear,* but Verdi became deterred by the text's intricacy and bold extremities; he hesitated and announced that he considered himself too old to undertake what he considered a monumental challenge.

Macbeth (1847), Verdi's seventh opera, was a rousing musico-dramatic success. In the opera, Verdi elevated the role of Shakespeare's Weird Sisters to that of the Witches, and captured a supernatural splendor in their music. In the title role, he introduced his new "high baritone," a new voice type that provided heretofore unknown possibilities for vocal expression. The new Verdi baritone possessed greater range, and as such, brought other vocal characterizations into sharper contrast and focus. Lady Macbeth became the dominant character in the opera: her Sleepwalking scene becoming a climax of the work that transformed Shakespeare's scene of recollection into a moment of grand operatic expression.

Verdi composed *Otello* almost a half century after *Macbeth.* He considered Shakespeare's *Othello* a high tragedy with consummate colossal power, perhaps the best constructed and most vividly theatrical of all of his dramas: a work that essentially progressed with no sub-plots, no episodes that fail to bear on the central action, and one in which all of its action focused toward its central dramatic core and purpose.

Boito's challenge in writing the libretto for *Otello* involved the inherent necessity to condense and transform the drama's complex elements into broader and simpler contexts. Shakespeare's hero is multi-faceted: he possesses a nihilistic "nature" combined with combinations of the heroic, the demonic, and the innocently pure. The Verdi-Boito *Otello* became an ambivalent, two-sided hero: a man of lofty, heroic nobility, who then transforms into a psychopathic, collapsing soul, ultimately plunging himself into exaggerated savagery. Verdi's music emphasizes the conflict of the defeated hero: Otello is a courageous man of great deed whose ultimate tragedy becomes his loss of glory and honor. Boito's prose portrays Otello as a profound, soul-searching man, who suffers from internal psychological conflict: a struggling victim who has lost love and respect, and self-destructs from hubris, pride, and arrogance. Verdi's music is saturated with glory and grandeur, and many times, directly opposed to Boito's words which express the hero's deeper, psychological turmoil.

For *Otello's* libretto, Boito challenged Shakespeare's 3500 lines of prose and condensed them to 700 lines, a task he brilliantly achieved while at the same time retaining the complete essence of the original drama. Boito omitted Shakespeare's Act I Venetian scene, in which Brabantio, Desdemona's father, accuses Othello of seducing his daughter. Othello eloquently defends himself: "She loved me for the dangers I had passed, and I loved her that she did pity them." Boito salvaged Shakespeare's magnificent prose by ingeniously incorporating its essence into the intensely romantic and passionate Act I Love Duet of Otello and Desdemona. There, Otello speaks of his pride in winning Desdemona's love, "E tu m'amavi le miei sventure," Boito altering the pronoun "she" to "you" so that in the opera text, Otello's words to Desdemona become, "You loved me for the dangers I had passed, and I loved you that you did pity them." Desdemona responds, repeating the phrase in the first person, "I loved you for the dangers you had passed...."

The opera portrays the hero's agonizing path to destructive jealousy, his doubts about himself and his marriage, and his road to psychopathic savagery. In Verdi's opera, Desdemona's characterization is transformed from Shakespeare's original: she is not characterized as Shakespeare's brave and willful woman who dared to enter into an unorthodox marriage. In Verdi, Desdemona is transformed into a naïve image of purity, innocence, and utterly devoted love — she is surrounded by music that bears an almost saintly connotation, a semi-divine, angelic image that reaches its apex in the Ave Maria.

The opera builds incessantly on Iago's poison, his "green monster" which Verdi provides a haunting musical leitmotif. Iago is the demonic figure of the drama: he forms a striking contrast to Otello's heroism and Desdemona's purity. Iago's diabolic motivations are brilliantly established in this Verdi-Boito creation, with composer and librettist adding a completely un-Shakespearean Credo — the laws of heresy in Shakespeare's times forbade specific Christian references in the theater.

Shakespeare's tragedy of *Othello* provided Verdi with the theatrical arena to breathe life into the moral issue of good and evil, what he believed was humanity's archetypal, eternal moral struggle. The virtues of good are represented by Desdemona, the faithful, virtuous, and loyal wife of Otello: its counter-force is Iago, the epitome of psychopathic evil. Otello himself becomes the battlefield in which the forces of good and evil collide and conflict. In the end, the essence of the tragedy is that the forces of evil become the victors, and evil claims the warrior's soul.

Verdi assured a place for Shakespeare in the opera house with *Macbeth* (1847), but most assuredly, with *Otello,* a tour de force that triumphantly premiered 40 years later. After the success of *Otello,* Verdi became rejuvenated, inspired, and motivated. During his entire career, he contemplated a comedy; perhaps, with Boito, he had found his inspiration.

Boito and Verdi had yet another Shakespearean gem to bring to the opera stage: *Falstaff.*

Fifty-three years had passed since Verdi composed a comic opera. His second opera, *Un Giorno di Regno,* (1840), "A King for a Day," also titled, *Il Finto Stanislao,* "The False Stanislaus," was Verdi's comic work until *Falstaff,* his last opera.

Un Giorno di Regno was composed at great speed; it was an unqualified disaster, and was withdrawn after only one performance. The action of the opera was set near Brest during the early 18th century. Belfiore, a Parisian officer, poses as King Stanislaus of Poland in order to protect the King from harm; he acted as a decoy while the real Stanislaus attempted to secure his throne. Disguised as the King, Belfiore visits Baron Kelbar's castle and helps his daughter, Giulietta, unite with her true lover, Edoardo, by removing her unwanted betrothed, Edoardo's uncle, the state Treasurer, La Rocca. At the same time, Belfiore reconciles with his true love, the Marchesa del Poggio, who thought he had abandoned her.

Stylistically, *Un Giorno di Regno* was a sentimental, light comedy possessing strong influences of Rossini and Donizetti. In retrospect, the opera must be judged as an unfortunate interlude in Verdi's progress, even though stylistically, it contained glimpses of that vital individuality that was to emerge so decisively in his future works. In contemporary reviews, as well as in Verdi's later recollections, its failure had as much to do with the poor quality of the performance, its poor libretto, and its underlying music.

The opera's failure coincided with traumatic events in Verdi's life. Verdi's two children had recently died, and in June 1840, three months before the completion and premiere of *Un Giorno di Regno,* his wife Margherita died. Verdi made every attempt possible to be released from his contract, but he was forced to return to Milan from Busetto in the midst of his terrible sorrows and oversee the production of his comic opera.

Comic opera, or opera buffa, required delicacy and grace, musical and dramatic qualities Verdi seemed to be lacking at that time. There is little imaginative scoring, and he found difficulty sustaining numbers that were so emphatically separated by unaccompanied or dry recitative, or "secco."

This attempt at opera buffa was clumsy: the public whistled and jeered, and critics wrote with varying degrees of pity and contempt. They considered the work an insipid comedy. Nevertheless, some critics were compassionate and recognized Verdi's tragic personal circumstances: the young composer had been forced to complete a work of gaiety at a time when he was heartbroken and experiencing a cruel and unexpected catastrophe that had struck his innermost soul. In effect, *Un Giorno di Regno,* Verdi's second operatic venture, fell far short of the expectations aroused by the first, *Oberto.* Ironically, five years after its failed premiere, the comic opera that had been hissed off the La Scala stage became a surprising success at Teatro San Benedetto (1859), the comedy theater in Venice, and later at San Carlo, Naples. Both *Oberto* and *Un Giorno di Regno* are rarely performed in the standard repertory of today's contemporary opera theaters, but when performed, it is more for curiosity rather than for operatic merit.

One can only speculate as to how much of the composer's bereavement or the pressures of time contributed to the comedy's failure. Nevertheless, its failure represented a bitter moment in Verdi's career, and the wound take a long time to heal. Ironically, with the phenomenal success of his first opera, *Oberto,* Verdi had literally become "King for a Day": with his opera actually titled "King for a Day," his career seemed to be over. In bitterness and resentment, Verdi swore that he would never again compose a comic opera, but more emphatically, at the time, he was ready to quit opera composing entirely.

Nevertheless, Verdi was lured back to his destiny after he was presented with the libretto for *Nabucco:* he stared at the prose lines of the Hebrew exile, "Va pensiero sull'ali dorati," and became struck by intense lyricism. In the end, Verdi's operatic pen could not be silenced. In later reminiscence, he said, "With this opera (*Nabucco*) my artistic career may be said to have begun."

Verdi's ambition to compose a comedy haunted him throughout his career, however, he never found the libretto that would stimulate his muse. In truth, he indeed wanted to vindicate the failure of *Un Giorno di Regno,* and certainly wanted to prove that he was capable of composing a comedy.

Verdi would fulfill his dream, and that illusive comedy would indeed become his final work: a comedy based on the works of his favorite poet, William Shakespeare, the opera based on the plays, *Henry IV* and *The Merry Wives of Windsor.*

Sir John Falstaff, appears in four of Shakespeare's plays: he is perhaps one of the most comic character creations in all English literature.

Shakespeare reputedly modeled Falstaff after Sir John Oldcastle, a soldier and martyred leader. In his first version of *Henry IV, Part One* (1597), Shakespeare called the comic character Sir John Oldcastle, but he was later forced to change the name after Oldcastle's descendants, prominent at the court, protested and threatened litigation.

Shakespeare then turned to Sir John Fastolf (1378 — 1459), an English career soldier who fought and made his fortune in the second phase of the Hundred Years' War between England and France (1337—1453). Fastolf served with distinction against the French at Agincourt (1415), Verneuil (1424), and in the Battle of the Herrings at Rouvay (1429), where he is reputed to have used herring barrels to shield his troops. Later, after his forces were defeated at Patay (1429), he was accused of cowardice, but he was subsequently cleared of the charge. In 1440 he retired from military service.

Shakespeare was able to document much of Fastolf's life and irascible personality through papers he left with a Norfolk friend. Fastolf was an acquisitive man, utterly ruthless in his business dealings, and being childless, leaving his possessions to the University of Oxford, which used them as their financial source for the new Magdalen College.

Shakespeare's *Henry IV, Part One* (1597) is the second in a sequence of four history plays: *Richard II, Henry IV, Part One, Henry IV, Part Two,* and *Henry V* — each play deals with an aspect of the power struggle between the houses of Lancaster and York. By creating Sir John Falstaff (Fastolf), Shakespeare added an element of comedy to the somber tone of the plays.

The history plays follow the deposition of King Richard II and are set in a kingdom plagued with rebellion, treachery, and shifting alliances. The two parts of *Henry IV* focus on Prince Hal, later to become Henry V, and his development and maturity from young spendthrift, idler, and loafer, to prudent ruler. As *Part One* begins, Henry IV laments the cowardice and frivolous life of his son, who, with his thriving rogue cronies, the fat and boisterous Falstaff and his red-nosed sidekick, Bardolph, drink and play childish pranks at Mistress Quickly's inn at Eastcheap.

In the next segment, *Henry IV, Part Two,* Prince Hal aids his father in war and proves his valor in battle. He kills the rebel Hotspur in personal combat, and compassionately laments the wasteful death of his noble opponent while his cowardly companion, Falstaff, lies on the ground nearby feigning death. After Prince Hal becomes King Henry V, he transforms; he rejects Falstaff and chides him for his malingering and drunkenness, ultimately banishing him.

In *The Merry Wives of Windsor* (1600), Shakespeare's Sir John Falstaff appears again, this time resurrected but reduced to a dissolute and clowning character — an opportunistic seducer involved in comic and romantic misadventures. According to unsupported tradition, *Merry Wives* was written by Shakespeare at the express command of Queen Elizabeth I who had had expressed her wish to see Falstaff in love.

In *Merry Wives*, Falstaff attempts to seduce Mistresses Page and Ford, two married women whose financial substance he covets. He shares his plan with his comrades, Bardolph, Pistol, and Nym, but after Falstaff discharges the services of Pistol and Nym, they betray him and reveal his scheme to the husbands of Mistresses Page and Ford.

After the wives compare their identical love letters from Falstaff, they resolve to trick the "greasy knight." Falstaff is twice humiliated by the wives: first he is dumped into a muddy ditch, and later, with the women disguised as witches, he is beaten. The trickery of the two women also serves to frustrate the jealous behavior of Master Ford.

The play's secondary plot concerns the wooing of the Pages' charming daughter, Anne, whose affection is the object of 3 rival suitors: Dr. Caius, Slender, and Fenton. With great comic effect, all three suitors employ Mistress Quickly, Caius' servant, to act as an intermediary to argue their case to young Anne. Slender is favored by Master Page; Mistress Page favors Caius as a son-in-law and devises a similar plan.

The final scene is a masquerade in which the plotters fully trick and humiliate Falstaff. Falstaff expects a rendezvous with Alice Ford and appears in a ridiculous disguise complete with stag's horns. The women and their husbands appear as witches and frighten and tease Falstaff. The marriage plans conceived by the Page's become foiled when Anne elopes with Fenton, the suitor of her choice. In the end, all identities are revealed, and in an atmosphere of good sport, Fenton is welcomed into the Page family and Falstaff is forgiven.

Many scholars are chagrined at Shakespeare's denigration of the courageous *Henry IV* Falstaff character into the ridiculed and humiliated Falstaff of *Merry Wives:* in the latter, his nobility becomes transformed into a pale reflection of his former self — a victim of indignities and an almost sado-masochistic farce that erupts into a pathetic carnival of humiliation and rejection that cause him to be baffled, duped, beaten, burnt, pricked, mocked, insulted, and perhaps worst of all, repentant.

Verdi's muse was essentially tragic, but composing a comedy opera was the fulfillment of a cherished ambition. Two years after the miraculous success of *Otello*, the directors of La Scala suggested that he compose a comic opera based on Cervantes's *Don Quixote*, but Verdi refused, content to remain at Sant'Agata and occupy himself with the life of a farmer and country affairs: in particular, he was preoccupied with the building of a hospital, reducing rents on his farms, improving properties with new irrigation systems, and in general, combating the depression in the area by developing employment.

Boito sent him the synopsis of a proposed libretto to be called *Falstaff*, based primarily on Shakespeare's *The Merry Wives of Windsor.* Immediately, Verdi's enthusiasm was aroused: he had finally found the comic libretto that he had dreamed of all of his life. Boito's inventions enthralled and dazzled him and he could not suppress his delight: "What a joy to be able to tell the public, here we are again! Come and see us!" The 80 year-old composer became rejuvenated and resilient, and the idea of *Falstaff* breathed new life into his creative spirits. Boito would become Verdi's catalyst and provide him with that necessary emotional scope to compose his music.

Nevertheless, Verdi had reservations and concerns about his advancing age, the fatigue he would necessarily encounter, and his frequent bouts of depression that had arisen after the deaths of so many of his dear friends. Boito became Verdi's gadfly, admonishing him that becoming immersed in laughter and comedy would exhilarate his mind, body, and spirit: a tragedy causes its author genuinely to suffer because one's thoughts undergo suggestions of sadness which render the nerves morbidly sensitive: "There is only one way to end your career more splendidly than with *Otello*, and that is to end it with *Falstaff.*" Boito reassured him that with *Falstaff*, composed while in his 80th year, Verdi would prove to his critics, among them the now dead Rossini, that he could write with great wit and with an almost Mozartian subtlety. Verdi's confidence began to grow. After all, he had proven in the past that he could enliven tragedy with comic elements: there are indeed comic inventions in his previous operas, subtle rather than profound elements.

There had been other operatic attempts at Shakespeare's irascible rogue knight: Antonio Salieri's *Falstaff* (1799); Balfe's *Falstaff* (1838); and from Verdi's supposed arch-rival, Otto Nicolai's *Die lustigen Weiber von Windsor* (1849), a bubbling and sparkling Rossini-like opera buffa.

Verdi was ready to attack comedy. He had all the ammunition he needed: Shakespeare and Boito. Boito not only served to rejuvenate Verdi, but he infected him. He provided Verdi with a concentrated, highly literary, beautifully balanced and paced, sparkling comic libretto. Verdi became inspired to illuminate the story of "Fatpaunch" in music, proving again that he possessed ingenious technical skill and musical inventiveness.

Verdi knew from experience that only a librettist with Boito's intellectual range could understand and transcend Shakespeare's nuances in order to transform *Merry Wives* for the operatic medium. For Verdi, the essence of the comic Falstaff character was for him to emerge in rich magnificence and splendor — only Boito, with his extraordinary fondness and talent for word-play and irony, was capable of achieving those results.

In meeting those expectations, Boito took many liberties with the Falstaff character. He adapted and synthesized his underlying story scenario from both *The Merry Wives of Windsor* and the *Henry IV* plays, extracting the poor jokes, and turning bad ones into excellent verse.

Verdi accepted Boito's libretto almost without alteration. Verdi was enthralled with the characterization of Falstaff: an archetype and loveable fat scoundrel and rogue who amusingly indulges in mischief. The humorous keystone of the plot was captivating: the fat knight's assault on the virtue of two rich tradesmen's wives with a view to helping himself to their husbands' money.

Verdi made it clear that Falstaff would be quite different from any opera he had ever written: *Falstaff* was the comedy he had wanted to compose all his life but had been prevented from for lack of the right libretto — and above all, with Falstaff, he would make himself laugh.

Boito, as he did in *Otello,* faced the challenge of simplifying the play's structure: he had to produce a leaner plot that contained no unnecessary characters that would clutter the action. His basic plot retains two major episodes from Shakespeare's *Merry Wives*: the laundry basket scene, and the intrigue and disguise in the forest. However, with much persuasion from Verdi, he charmingly developed the romantic subplot of the lovers, Nannetta and Fenton, a romance that brings the plot into the world of opera — a world of stolen love that Verdi underscored with beautiful love duets, prompting Boito to describe the Nannetta-Fenton episodes as "sprinkled like sugar on a tart."

In paring down the number of characters, Boito dispensed with Justice Shallow and his stupid nephew, Sir Hugh Evans, Nym, and even Mr. Page. As a result, Mistress Page takes the spotlight as a freelance intriguer, while Nannetta (Anne Page) becomes one from the Ford family; her two unwelcome suitors are only Fenton and Dr. Caius. Boito's excisions and alterations are almost without exception beautifully judged, causing the plot to move forward with a tighter and more focused cast of characters.

In many respects, *Falstaff,* which represents a fusion of three Shakespeare plays, possesses more subtlety than its models. Shakespeare, particularly in *Merry Wives,* provides a comedy involving much trickery, deception, and a series of humiliations, with its farcical episodes containing threads of malice and cruelty. Verdi's opera offers a more rambunctious and happier world than Shakespeare's, in which deception and trickery seem to be relished for the sheer joy of intriguing and plotting. In the opera, no one seems to take Falstaff's offences very seriously: Falstaff is not so much the victim of deceit and trickery as the cause of fun, frolic, and laughter, all of which ultimately resolves into forgiveness, tolerance, and a world full of loving harmony.

In *Falstaff's* music, Verdi most assuredly departs from traditions that had been the cornerstone of his art. *Falstaff's* musical focus is not on extensive thematic development of conventional arias, duets and trios, or in ensembles packed with drama, emotion, or psychological development: those conventions are sparse throughout the score, with the rare exceptions of Ford's aria, "È sogno," and the short romantic duets between Nannetta and Fenton.

In character, *Falstaff's* music is light and airy, bubbly, delicate, episodic, and possesses an almost seamless accumulation of clever, fragmentary musical inventions, all of which dutifully follow the mercurial quality of the libretto. Verdi proves that he is a supreme craftsman: the music possesses a combination of brilliance, classical purity, gracefulness, clarity of construction, and tenderness, with explosions that are humorous and witty, but never extravagant or vulgar.

The score — particularly in the ensembles — is saturated with scherzos (a sprightly and humorous compositional form in rapid tempo), and fugues (two or more themes developed with a continuous interweaving of their vocal parts). Most of the scherzos and fugues appear during the concerted finales of each act: comic inventions that are composed with brevity, clarity, and organic unity, that require excellent acting-singers who possess clear diction and deft verbal and musical attack in order to convey their comic essence.

Verdi scatters a profusion of ingenious melodic inventions throughout the score, fragments that become memorable melodic leitmotifs: Falstaff's "Honor" monologue; Quickly's absurd "reverenza" and "povera donna," and her interplay with Falstaff on "dalle due alle tre"; and Falstaff's explosion of ecstasy, "Caro Signor Fontana." But there are indeed arias, very short one: Falstaff's endearingly smug aria of self-love, "Va vecchio John," his wooing of Alice Ford, "Quand erò paggio del Duca di Norfolk," and Ford's jealous explosion, "È sogno," a serious introspective moment in which he explores the dramatic ambiguity of his feelings.

Falstaff is a wonder of the opera world, an outpouring from a true master of music drama who ended his career with an ingenious masterpiece that take its rightful place beside other great comic operas: Mozart's *The Marriage of Figaro,* Wagner's *Die Meistersinger,* and Rossini's *The Barber of Seville.*

Falstaff's success is a tribute to Verdi's genius and versatility. It is an opera that combines the beauty, subtlety, wit, and wisdom of Mozart's three great Italian operas, with an almost Beethoven-like chamber music delicacy in its orchestral expression.

Shaw noted that "It is not often that a man's strength is so immense that he can remain an athlete after bartering half of it to old age for experience; but the thing happens occasionally, and need not so greatly surprise us in Verdi's case."

The premiere of *Falstaff* took place at La Scala almost six years to the day of *Otello's* premiere. Inevitably, it became an immediate and huge triumph, a national and international sensation.

Verdi was delighted that it escaped being called Wagnerian, although today it is spoken of in the same breath as Wagner's considerably heavier and longer comedy, *Die Meistersinger.* Richard Strauss, a man who had for many years worshipped at the Bayreuth shrine, declared *Falstaff* to be one of the masterpieces of all time.

After Verdi completed the final act, he accompanied it with a note to Ricordi, paraphrasing a passage in Boito's libretto:

"Tutto è finito, Va, va, vecchio John. Cammina per la tua via fi che tu puoi. Vicertente tupe di briccone eternamente vero sotto Maschera diversa in ogni tempo, in ogni luogo. Va, va, cammina, cammina, Addio."

"It is all finished. Go, go, old John. Go on your way for as long as you can. Amusing rogue, forever true beneath the masks you wear in different times and places. Go, go, on your way. Farewell."

Falstaff possesses timeless humor and gaiety: it captures the golden warmth and ironic laughter of Verdi's old age — a magnificent operatic comic farewell from the master of operatic tragedy.

Principal Characters in Falstaff

Sir John Falstaff, a knight	Baritone
Bardolph, a cohort	Tenor
Pistol, a cohort	Tenor
Ford, a wealthy burgher	Baritone
Alice Ford, his wife	Soprano
Nannetta Ford, their daughter	Soprano
Fenton, Nannetta's suitor	Tenor
Dr. Caius, another suitor	Tenor
Meg Page, a neighbor	Soprano
Dame Quickly, servant of Dr. Caius	Soprano

Servants, citizens of Windsor, masqueraders, witches and fairies

TIME: Fifteenth century
PLACE: Windsor, England, during the reign of Henry IV

Brief Story Synopsis

Sir John Falstaff contrives a preposterous plan to relieve his diminishing financial resources: he will lure Mistresses Alice Ford and Meg Page, two of the wealthy Windsor wives, into love affairs.

He sends each of the wives identical letters that offers his love.

However, the wives realize his duplicity; they scorn his impudence, and plot to teach him a lesson.

Ford learns about Falstaff's insidious plan to seduce his wife, anad seething with jealousy, devises his own intrigue to avenge the wily knight.

Disguised as Mr. Fontana, Ford beseeches Falstaff to help him win Alice Ford's favors.

Dame Quickly advises Falstaff that Alice Ford ecstatically anticipates a rendezvous with him. Falstaff's rendezvous with Alice is interrupted by the avenging Ford and his cohorts. Fearing that Falstaff will be discovered, the wives hide Falstaff in a laundry basket. Afterwards, all watch as the basket is dumped into the Thames River.

The wives contrive another intrigue intended to humiliate Falstaff. Dame Quickly convinces him that Alice still yearns for his love.

A rendezvous is arranged at Windsor Park. All the conspirators — wives and husbands — await Falstaff with the intension of humbling Sir John. In the end, they beat, castigate, and denounce him.

Peace is finally made after Ford and Sir John Falstaff confess that they have become victims of their own folly.

Story Narrative with Music Highlight Examples

Act I – Scene 1: a room in the Garter Inn

At the Garter Inn, Falstaff, a jovial, fat rogue, quaffs huge drafts while he busily seals two letters: looking on are his rowdy and rambunctious cohorts, Bardolph and Pistol. Falstaff has conjured up a plan to alleviate the low state of his financial resources, and has written identical letters to Mistresses Page and Ford, the wives of two wealthy burghers with whom he hopes to conclude a profitable liaison.

The contentious Dr. Caius arrives and immediately quarrels with Falstaff, claiming that his depraved friends, Bardolph and Pistol, got him drunk the night before, picked his pockets, thrashed his servants, and stole two of his horses. After an exchange of furious insults, Pistol and Dr. Caius duel mockingly. Falstaff calmly dismisses the humiliated Dr. Caius, who, solemnly promises never again to drink in the presence of such scoundrels.

Falstaff, feigning virtue and morality, admonishes his colleagues about their future behavior: "Steal politely, and at the appropriate."

Rubar con garbo e a tempo

Falstaff orders Bardolph and Pistol to deliver his love letters respectively to Mistresses Ford and Page: his rogue accomplices refuse, claiming that to partake in such an insidious plan would be beneath their integrity and honor. Undaunted, Falstaff calls a page to deliver the letters.

Falstaff is exasperated by his cohorts' betrayal: he rebukes them in an ironical sermon filled with sarcasm and mock pomposity; a scathing harangue about honor that condemns them as "cloache d'ignominia" ("sewers of ignominy").

L'Onore!

Defiantly, Falstaff takes a broom and sweeps the two men from the Garter Inn.

Act I – Scene 2: a Garden outside the Ford house.

In a mood of gaiety and good humor, Mistress Page and Dame Quickly join Alice Ford and her daughter, Nannetta.

The Merry Wives:

Meg Page and Alice Ford compare the presumptuous letters they have just received from Sir John Falstaff: they discover that the letters are identical:

Fulgida Alice! Amor t'offro..
"Resplendent Alice! I offer you love.."

Fulgida Meg! Amor t'offro..
"Resplendent Meg! I offer you love."

Facciamo il paio

The wives erupt into uncontrolled laughter, and then scorn the knight's impudence by planning a revenge that will teach the audacious knight a lesson.

The men arrive, Ford (Alice's husband), Fenton (seeking to marry Ford's daughter, Nannetta), Dr. Caius (a suitor whom Ford prefers for Nannetta), and Bardolph and Pistol, the latter seeking revenge against Falstaff for humiliating them: Bardolph and Pistol have betrayed Falstaff and exposed his plan to seduce the Windsor wives to Mr. Ford.

The men leave to plot their intrigue, but Fenton and Nannetta remain behind and romance each other: Nannetta is disturbed and perplexed because her father has arranged for her to marry the contemptible Dr. Caius.

Labbra di foco! Labbra di fiori!

The wives conspire to launch their intrigue against Falstaff: they decide to send Dame Quickly to Falstaff with a message advising the knight that Alice Ford has consented to his offer: thus, they will lure Falstaff to the Ford house and deal with him accordingly.

Unbeknownst to the wives, the men have contrived their own intrigue to trap Falstaff: Ford will meet Falstaff in disguise and with an assumed name, and he will lure Falstaff to his house and exact unmerciful punishment on him.

Act II – Scene 1: at the Garter Inn

Bardolph and Pistol, with feigned sincerity offer chest-beating penance, a sign of their begging Falstaff to forgive them and restore them to his good graces.

Siam pentiti e contriti

Dame Quickly is announced: she bows to Falstaff and addresses him as "reverenza" ("Your reverence"), a subtly mocking allusion which flatters the naïve knight to distraction.

Reverenza

Dame Quickly advises Falstaff that Alice is a hapless woman: he has awakened her desires, and she is desperate for his love; a "Povera donna" ("Poor woman"). Quickly arranges for Falstaff to meet Alice at her home, but only when her violently jealous husband is away: "dalle due alle tre" ("Between two and three"); Falstaff repeats the time of the appointment with lecherous zeal.

Dalle due alle tre

After Dame Quickly departs, Falstaff expresses his self- satisfaction, confident that his personal charm and dashing elan will make his amorous adventure with Alice Ford a raging success.

Va vecchio John

Bardolph announces that a stranger desires to make Falstaff's acquaintance: he is a *Signor Fontana.* (Mr. Ford in disguise: Mr. Brook in Shakespeare). He has expressed his gratitude by bringing Falstaff a gift of a large bottle of Cyprus wine.

Caro signor Fontana!

Without hesitation, Falstaff excitedly accepts *Signor Fontana's* commission, exacerbating Ford by telling him casually that he already has an appointment with Mistress Ford: "dalle due alle tre," the afternoon hours when her husband is always away. Falstaff, exhilarated by his new role as intermediary for the despairing *Signor Fontana*, prides his new role: "Te lo cornifico" ("I am a cuckold for you"). Falstaff excuses himself: he goes off to dress himself in his best attire.

Alone, Ford becomes perplexed and bewildered, unable to believe that his wife is deceptive and unfaithful: "È sogno" ("It is a dream"). Then he erupts into rage, condemning the institution of marriage and demonic women: he vows his determination to seek vengeance.

O matrimonio: Inferno!

Falstaff returns, arrayed in his most exquisite finery. As both exit arm-in-arm, they exchange elaborate courtesies and exaggerated politeness: the knight is elated as he contemplates his forthcoming victory; Ford, behind feigned smiles, fumes in agonized rage.

Act II – Scene 2: a room in Ford's house

Dame Quickly provides a detailed report about her meeting with Falstaff to Mistresses Ford and Page, ridiculing Falstaff as she repeats the time of the appointment: "dalle due alle tre."

The wives prepare for the arrival of their victim: servants place a large laundry basket near a window and are advised that when called, they are to empty the basket in the river. Nannetta interrupts the busy preparations to tearfully report to her mother that her father insists that she marry the repulsive Dr. Caius. Mistress Alice Ford, sympathetic and understanding of her daughter's dilemma, assures her that she will intervene and do everything to contravert her father's wishes.

Falstaff is announced. All hide, leaving Mistress Alice Ford sitting calmly in a chair with her lute. Falstaff wastes no time in pursuing his courtship of Alice. As he woos her, he excuses his obesity: "Quand'ero paggio del Duca di Norfolk" ("When I was the page to the Duke of Norfolk"), a boast about his youth when "I was so slim, so supple and so agile, that I could have slipped through the eye of a sewing needle."

Quand'ero paggio del Duca di Norfolk

Just as the rogue knight's courtship of Alice is about to approach intimacy, Dame Quickly announces the imminent arrival of a distraught and agitated Meg Page: Falstaff quickly hides behind a screen. Meg announces that Ford is en route: he is insanely jealous, convinced that Alice has a lover concealed in the house, and is determined to expose him.

Ford arrives, accompanied by Fenton, Dr. Caius, Bardolph, Pistol, and other co-conspirators. Ford suspects that Falstaff is hiding in the laundry basket: he opens the basket, flings all the dirty linen over the floor, but does not find Falstaff. In frustration, he and the men proceed to search another part of the house where they expect to find the rakish knight.

After the men leave, Falstaff emerges from behind the screen, and the women hurriedly conceal him in the large laundry basket, pile soiled clothes over him, and fasten the lid. During the commotion, Nannetta and Fenton are unnoticed as they quietly hide behind a screen. A moment later, Ford and his cohorts return, this time more furious and more determined than ever to find the rakish knight.

As all stand frozen in silence, a loud kiss resounds from behind a screen: Ford is elated, convinced that he has finally caught the evasive Falstaff. The men advance toward the screen, prepared to pounce on the knight with full fury; the women's laughter muffles Falstaff's cries; he is suffocating from his confinement in the laundry basket.

The men overturn the screen, and to their amazement, they discover Fenton and Nannetta, the unsuspecting lovers stealing a moment of love, and oblivious to all the commotion surrounding them. Ford, frustrated again, becomes more enraged than ever, rebukes Fenton, and orders him from his house. Suddenly, Bardolph announces that he sees Falstaff outside: Ford and the men rush out in pursuit.

With the men gone, Mistress Ford summons her servants, who, with a huge effort, lift the laundry basket up to the window and throw it into the Thames which flows below. Ford returns, delighted as he witnesses Falstaff climbing clumsily from the water: their revenge achieved, all erupt into a riotous fanfare of triumph.

Act III – Scene 1: in front of the Garter Inn

As the sun sets, Falstaff returns to the Garter Inn: disgruntled, sad, disillusioned, bemoaning his disgrace and humiliation, and reviling the wickedness of the world. He orders a glass of hot wine, gulps it down, and then recounts the outrageous treatment he received from the Windsor wives. Gradually, the wine overcomes him, reviving his faith in himself: his spirits, courage, and ego become rejuvenated. Suddenly, Dame Quickly appears before him: she bears another message from Alice, but Falstaff rebuffs her, her repeated "reverenzas" transforming him into vindictive fury. Dame Quickly perseveres in restoring the knight's confidence in her: she appeals to Falstaff's vulnerability by assuring him of Alice's continuing affection for him.

Dame Quickly arranges another meeting between Falstaff and Mistress Ford: at midnight, they will meet at Herne's Oak in Windsor Park: he is to be disguised as the Black Huntsman, the "Black Knight" whose ghost reputedly haunts the spot. Both enter the Inn to discuss their plans in a more private setting.

However, all the conspirators have been eavesdropping on their conversation: Alice, Meg, Nannetta, Ford, Fenton, and Dr. Caius. The plotters unite and decide they will exact their final revenge on Falstaff: they will terrify the unsuspecting Falstaff wearing the disguises of fairies, elves, and devils.

Ford and Dr. Caius conspire another intrigue. Caius will disguise himself in monk's robes, and Nannetta will be veiled in white: they will marry that very night, and Ford will bless the union. However, Dame Quickly has overheard their intrigue and vows to stop them: she runs off to advise Alice Ford and Nannetta about their plot.

Act III – Scene 2: Herne's Oak in Windsor Park. On a moonlit night, all the conspirators appear in disguises.

Fenton intones a serenade to Nannetta.

Dal labbro il canto

Nannetta arrives and they embrace. Alice Ford and Dame Quickly are determined to upset Ford's plans to have Dr. Caius marry Nannetta: they give Fenton a monk's disguise to wear.

Falstaff appears, wearing two stag horns and an enormous cloak. After he solemnly counts the 12 bells of midnight, Nannetta is heard invoking the fairies in song.

Sul fil d'un soffio etesio

Alice Ford appears, and Falstaff immediately makes awkward attempts to embrace and romance her: Alice dissuades him, cautioning him that Meg is close behind. Indeed, Meg suddenly appears to warn them that a pack of witches is pursuing her: Alice flees in mock terror.

Nannetta and spirits appear, Meg disguised as a Green Nymph, Pistol as a satyr, and children dressed as imps and fairies. All dance around Falstaff: they thrash and kick him, and then condemn him as an "impure mortal," all the while shouting "pizzica, pizzica" ("Pinch and bite him.).Falstaff is scared out of his senses and transforms into frightful fear: he believes he will be doomed if he gazes on supernatural beings, and throws himself face down on the ground, all the while promising that he will mend his ways.

Suddenly, Bardolph's hood accidentally slips off. Falstaff recognizes him, and the entire charade is unmasked. Falstaff assumes a new stature, philosophically accepting his humiliation with rueful good humor. In Shakespeare's *Merry Wives*, Falstaff laments, "I do begin to perceive that I am made an ass," and in Henry IV, Part One, "they could not have had all this enjoyment without me," and "I am not only witty in myself, but the cause that wit is in other men."

Ford agreed to give his daughter, Nannetta, to Dr. Caius in marriage, but the women are determined to upset his plan. Dame Quickly disguises Bardolph as the Fairy Queen, dressing him in gown and veil: Dr. Caius joins the Fairy Queen (Bardolph), believing it is Nannetta. Fenton, wearing a monk's disguise, is joined with Nannetta. Alice Ford urges her husband, unaware of the real identities of the parties, to bless both pairs in a double marriage ceremony. After the marriage, everyone unmasks and the charade is exposed: the Fairy Queen, Bardolph in disguise, has been "married" to Dr. Caius, and the two young lovers, Fenton and Nannetta, have finally wed.

Ford accepts defeat graciously: Falstaff, humiliated, finds comfort that another has been the victim of ridicule.

All join in a tribute to man's foolishness: "Tutto nel mondo è burla" ("Everything in the world is a joke").

Tutto il mondo é burla.

Even a fool, when he holdeth his peace, is counted wise. Proverbs 17:28

Libretto

Act I — Scene 1
A room in the Garter Inn. Falstaff is busy at a candle flame
where he is warming up the wax to seal two letters with a ring.
After they are sealed, he turns off the light and starts to drink comfortably.

Dr. Cajus:
Falstaff!

Dr. Caius: *(entering)*
Falstaff!

Falstaff:
Olà!

Falstaff: *(calling to a waiter)*
Oho!

Dr. Cajus:
Sir John Falstaff!

Dr. Caius:
Sir John Falstaff!

Bardolfo:
Oh! che vi piglia?

Bardolph: *(to Caius)*
Why all the shouting?

Dr. Cajus:
Hai battuto i miei servi!

Dr. Caius:
You assaulted my servants!

Falstaff:
Oste! un'altra bottiglia di Xeres.

Falstaff: *(paying no attention)*
Waiter! Some more of your sherry!

Dr. Cajus:
Hai fiaccata la mia giumenta baia,
sforzata la mia casa.

Dr. Caius:
You were poaching in my woods.
You broke in to my house.

Falstaff:
Ma non la tua massaia.

Falstaff:
But not your housekeeper.

Dr. Cajus:
Troppa grazia! Una vecchia cisposa.
Ampio messere,
se foste venti volte John Falstaff cavaliere,
v'obbligherò a rispondermi.

Dr. Caius:
How obliging! That befuddled old woman!
Sir High and Mighty!
If I was twenty times stronger,
I'd challenge you to answer me.

Falstaff:
Ecco la mia risposta:
ho fatto ciò che hai detto.

Falstaff:
No need to shout so loudly.
I did it all with pride and pleasure.

Dr. Cajus:
E poi?

Dr. Caius:
This is a case to settle in court.

Falstaff:
L'ho fatto apposta.

Falstaff:
Take my advice and forget it.

Dr. Cajus:
M'appellerò al consiglio real.

Dr. Caius: *(turning on Bardolph)*
Get some counsel!

Falstaff:
Vatti con dio.
Sta' zitto o avrai le beffe; quest'è il consiglio
mio.

Dr. Cajus:
Non è finita!

Falstaff:
Al diavolo!

Dr. Cajus:
Bardolfo!

Bardolfo:
Ser Dottore.

Dr. Cajus:
Tu, ier, m'hai fatto bere.

Bardolfo:
Pur troppo! e che dolore!
Sto mal. D'un tuo pronostico m'assisti.
Ho l'intestino guasto.
Malanno agli osti che dan la calce al vino!
Vedi questa meteora?

Dr. Cajus:
La vedo.

Bardolfo:
Essa si corca
rossa così ogni notte.

Dr. Cajus:
Pronostico di forca!
M'hai fatto ber, furfante, con lui, narrando
frasche;
poi, quando fui ben ciùschero, m'hai
vuotato le tasche.

Bardolfo:
Non io.

Dr. Cajus:
Chi fu?

Falstaff:
Go hang yourself.
Be quiet and avoid trouble, that's my
advice.

Dr. Caius:
It's not finished yet!

Falstaff:
Go to the devil!

Dr. Caius:
You, Bardolph!

Bardolph:
Learned doctor!

Dr. Caius:
Last night you got me drunk.

Bardolph:
Stupid me. I'm hung over. My headache!
I'll need professional help.
Even my guts are gutted.
The wine was poisoned with water!
Look here, my nose is shinier than ever?

Dr. Caius:
Like a beacon!

Bardolph:
Red as a torch by night,
like an ever-flaming fire.

Dr. Caius: *(indicating Pistol)*
To light you to the gallows.
You got me drunk, you scoundrel.
You're both so clever!
As soon as you saw me bleary-eyed,
Yes, you emptied my pockets.

Bardolph:
Who, me?

Dr. Caius: *(to Pistol)*
And you.

Falstaff:
Pistola!

Pistola:
Padrone.

Falstaff:
Hai tu vuotate
le tasche a quel messere?

Dr. Cajus:
Certo fu lui. Guardate.
Come s'atteggia al niego quel ceffo da
bugiardo!
Qui c'eran due scellini del regno d'Edoardo
e sei mezzecorone.
Non ne riman più segno.

Pistola:
Padron, chiedo di battermi con quest'arma
di legno.
Vi smentisco!

Dr. Cajus:
Bifolco! tu parli a un gentiluomo!

Pistola:
Gonzo!

Dr. Cajus:
Pezzente!

Pistola:
Bestia!

Dr. Cajus:
Can!

Pistola:
Vil!

Dr. Cajus:
Spauracchio!

Pistola:
Gnomo!

Falstaff:
Hey, Pistol!

Pistol:
What is it?

Falstaff:
Did you divest the doctor of some of his
trifles?

Dr. Caius:
Yes, he's the one! Observe him.
That ugly face speaks volumes:
It tells me he's a liar.
I had collectors' coins
that dated back to Edward,
six pieces, and not even one remaining.

Pistol: *(grabbing a broom)*
I'll sweep him out the door
for character assassination.
Sir, how dare you!

Dr. Caius:
You rubbish! You're speaking to a cavalier.

Pistol:
Donkey!

Dr. Caius:
You beggar!

Pistol:
Weasel!

Dr. Caius:
Leech!

Pistol:
Rat!

Dr. Caius:
You scarecrow!

Pistol:
Lizard!

Dr. Cajus:
Germoglio di mandragora!

Pistola:
Chi?

Dr. Cajus:
Tu.

Pistola:
Ripeti!

Dr. Cajus:
Sì!

Pistola:
Saette!

Falstaff:
Ehi là! Pistola!
Bardolfo! Chi ha vuotato le tasche a quel
messere?

Dr. Cajus:
Fu l'un dei due.

Bardolfo:
Costui beve, poi pe'l gran bere
perde i suoi cinque sensi, poi ti narra una
favola
ch'egli ha sognato mentre dormì sotto la
tavola.

Falstaff:
L'odi? Se ti capaciti, del ver tu sei sicuro.
I fatti son negati. Vattene in pace.

Dr. Cajus:.
Giuro
che se mai mi ubriaco ancora all'osteria
sarà fra gente onesta, sobria, civile e pia.

Bardolfo e Pistola:
Amen.

Falstaff:
Cessi l'antifona. La urlate in contrattempo.

Dr. Caius:
You feeble-minded parasite!

Pistol:
Me?

Dr. Caius:
You!

Pistol:
Repeat that.

Dr. Caius:
Yes!

Pistol:
By thunder!

Falstaff:
Hold on, you hotheads!
Come, let's avoid a scene, Bardolph!
Did you pick his pockets?

Dr. Caius:
They both are guilty!

Bardolph:
He was boozing, hitting the bottle
till he could barely stagger.
Now he's back with a fairy tale,
a flimsy fable he dreamed while he was
snoring under the table.

Falstaff:
Listen! You can't dispute this man's honesty.
Your charges stand refuted, so get along.

Dr. Caius: *(before departing)*
Monstrous! You'll never catch me again
inside this filthy stable, I'll confine my
drinking to pious church-going people!

Bardolph and Pistol::
Amen!

Falstaff:
Less liturgy! Your fervor needs refining.

L'arte sta in questa massima: «rubar con
garbo e a tempo».

The fine art of theft is delicate;
to steal requires charm and poise.

Siete dei rozzi artisti.

Where was your sense of timing?

«Sei polli: sei scellini,
trenta giarre di Xeres: due lire;
tre tacchini»

Six chickens: six shillings.
Thirty bottles of sherry: two florins!
Three capons.

Fruga nella mia borsa.
«Due fagiani, un'acciuga»

Take a look in my wallet.
Brace of pheasants, one anchovy.

Bardolfo:
Un mark, un mark, un penny.

Bardolph:
A mark, a mark, a farthing, next to nothing.

Falstaff:
Fruga.

Falstaff:
Shake it! Shake it!

Bardolfo:
Qui non c'è più uno spicciolo.

Bardolph:
I've shaken every penny out.

Falstaff:
Sei la mia distruzione!
Spendo ogni sette giorni dieci ghinee!
Beone!
So che se andiam, la notte, di taverna in
taverna,
quel tuo naso ardentissimo mi serve da
lanterna;
ma quel risparmio d'olio me lo consumi in
vino.
Son trent'anni che abbevero quel fungo
porporino!
Costi troppo.
E tu pure. Oste! un'altra bottiglia.

Falstaff:
You have led me to ruin,
costing a fortune
just to keep you in service.
You guzzler! Often we weave and wander.
Roam from tavern to tavern nightly,
guided by that flaming nose of yours
burning ever brightly, over there.
But what you save me in oil
you spend on sack and sherry.
Thirty years I've watered
that massive over-ripened berry.
(to Bardolph) Too expensive!
(to Pistol) You included!

Mi struggete le carni! Se Falstaff
s'assottiglia
non è più lui, nessuno più l'ama; in questo
addome
c'è un migliaio di lingue che annunciano il
mio nome!

Waiter! Some more of the finest!
All I've got you've devoured.
A Falstaff worn and wasted
is overlooked and under-valued.
As a noble by birth, a noble, I inspire the
masses to acclaim this global girth!

Pistola:
Falstaff immenso!

Pistol:
Falstaff stupendous!

Bardolfo:
Enorme Falstaff!

Bardolph:
Tremendous Falstaff!

Falstaff:
Quest'è il mio regno. Lo ingrandirò.
Ma è tempo d'assottigliar l'ingegno.

Falstaff: *(patting his abdomen)*
Here is my kingdom, and here I reign.
Today, we have to sharpen our wits.

Bardolfo e Pistola:
Assottigliam.

Bardolph and Pistol:
You give the word.

Falstaff:
V'è noto un tal, qui del paese,
che ha nome Ford?

Falstaff:
Perhaps you know a local burgher
by the name of Ford.

Bardolfo: e Pistola:
Sì.

Bardolph and Pistol:
Yes!

Falstaff:
Quell'uom è un gran borghese.

Falstaff:
A merchant born into prosperity.

Pistola:
Più liberal d'un Creso.

Pistol:
He's got more gold than Midas.

Bardolfo:
È un Lord!

Bardolph:
He's a Lord!

Falstaff:
Sua moglie è bella.

Falstaff:
His wife is a beauty.

Pistola:
E tien lo scrigno.

Pistol:
Who holds the purse strings.

Falstaff:
È quella! O amor! Sguardo di stella!
Collo di cigno! e il labbro? Un fior. Un fior
che ride.
Alice è il nome, e un giorno, come passar mi
vide
ne' suoi paraggi, rise. M'ardea l'estro
amatorio nel cor.
La dèa vibrava raggi di specchio ustorio,
su me, su me, sul fianco baldo, sul gran
torace,
sul maschio piè, sul fusto saldo, erto,
capace;

Falstaff:
Precisely! Ah, love! Those eyes that
sparkle! Her ample bosom!
Her two lips, a chalice!
Her name is Alice, a fragrant flower.
One morning, strolling along,
she saw me and lingered, nodding, smiling.
A flame of passion ignited my heart.
The goddess cast a radiant dart
that landed on me!
The stalwart shoulders, the massive torso,
On shapely legs, still more so on arms.
Ample, capacious.

e il suo desir in lei fulgea sì al mio congiunto
che parea dir: «Io son di Sir John Falstaff»

Bardolfo:
Punto.

Falstaff:
E a capo. Un'altra; e questa ha nome
Margherita.

Bardolfo e Pistola:
Un'altra.

Pistola:
La chiaman Meg.

Falstaff:
È anch'essa dei miei pregi invaghita.
E anch'essa tien le chiavi dello scrigno.
Costoro saran le mie Golconde e le mie
Coste d'oro!
Guardate. Io sono ancora una piacente
estate di san Martino.
A voi, due lettere infuocate.

Tu porta questa a Meg; tentiam la sua virtù.
Già vedo che il tuo naso arde di zelo.

E tu porta questa ad Alice.

Pistola:
Porto una spada al fianco.
Non sono un messer Pandarus. Ricuso.

Falstaff:
Saltimbanco.

Bardolfo:
Sir John, in questo intrigo non posso
accondiscendervi,
lo vieta...

Falstaff:
Chi?

Her eyes conveyed fire, and yearning, and
desire: "I'm yours alone, John Falstaff!"

Bardolph:
Unquote.

Falstaff:
There's also another: her name is
Margherita.

Bardolph and Pistol:
Another!

Pistol:
Or Meg for short.

Falstaff:
She has also felt my fatal fascination.
The darling also holds the purse strings.
Together, they'll be my West and East
Indies, my Eldorado.
My vessel goes sailing forth to one and
then the other to explore for treasure.
See here, two enterprising letters.

(to Bardolph)
Go, carry this to Meg. We'll test her virtue.
Your nose glows with zeal at the prospect.

(to Pistol)
And this you'll deliver to Alice.

Pistol:
I'll not dishonor my sword.
I'm no conniving go-between. No, never!

Falstaff:
Good for nothing!

Bardolph:
Sir John, in such deception
I as well cannot participate.
My conscience...

Falstaff:
Your what?

Bardolfo:
L'onore!

Bardolph:
Honor!

Falstaff:
Ehi! paggio!
Andate a impendervi,
ma non più a me!

Falstaff: *(to a passing page)*
Hey! Robin!
You can go hang. I'm through with both of
you!

(to a Page)

Due lettere, prendi, per due signore.
Consegna tosto, corri, via, lesto, va'!

Two letters for two fine ladies.
Hurry, run! Scamper! Go! Scurry! Go!

Falstaff proceeds to scold Bardolph and Pistol, broom in hand.

L'onore! Ladri!
Voi state ligi all'onor vostro, voi!
Cloache d'ignominia, quando, non sempre,
noi possiam star ligi al nostro.
Io stesso, sì, io, io!

Your honor! Scoundrels!
How dare you speak to me of honor?
You! You garbage from the sewers!
When even I at times have sacrificed my
conscience. Yes, even I, I, too! I, too!

Devo talor da un lato
porre il timor di dio e,
per necessità, sviar l'onore e usare
stratagemmi ed equivoci, destreggiar,
bordeggiare.

I have on rare occasions turned from the
eye of heaven: I have been forced to leave
the straight and narrow, to dabble in
skullduggery and subterfuge,
slight of hand, double-dealing.

E voi, coi vostri cenci
e coll'occhiata torta
da gattopardo
e i fetidi sghignazzi, avete a scorta
il vostro onor!

You foul and filthy rabble,
in ragged cast-off clothing,
with shifty glances,
you dare to smirk and simper
about your honor! Have you no pride?

Che onore? che onor? che onor! che ciancia!
Che baia! Può l'onore riempirvi la pancia?
No. Può l'onor rimettervi uno stinco?
Non può.
Né un piede? No. Né un dito? No. Né un
capello? No.
L'onor non è chirurgo. Ch'è dunque? Una
parola.
Che c'è in questa parola? C'è dell'aria che vola.
Bel costrutto! L'onore lo può sentire chi è
morto?

What honor? Go on, go on!
All bubble and babble.
Can your honor fill your belly when
empty? No!
And can honor mend a leg that's broken?
Oh, no!
An ankle? No! A finger? No! Or a whisker?
No!
So honor's not a surgeon. What is it?
Only a word, and what is it made of?
Only air floating onward. Handy dandy!

No. Vive sol coi vivi?
Neppure: perché a torto
lo gonfian le lusinghe,
lo corrompe l'orgoglio,
l'ammorban le calunnie;
e per me non ne voglio!

Ma, per tornare a voi, furfanti, ho atteso
troppo.
E vi discaccio.
Olà! lesti! lesti! al galoppo!
al galoppo! Il capestro assai bene vi sta.
Ladri! Via! Via di qua!
Via di qua! Via di qua!

This honor, does it endure hereafter? No!
Valued by the living? Unlikely!
Because inflated by flattery and fawning
or corrupted by envy, then swallowed up
by slander. I will have nothing of it, no!
I'll not have it, no, no!

But turning back to you, oh vipers!
I've been too indulgent;
the party's over!
Away! Faster, faster!
On the gallop, on the gallop!
Robber! Rascals! Vipers! Vermin!
Hurry up! Out of here!

Falstaff brandishes a broom, and sweeps Bardolph and Pistol from the Garter Inn.

Act I — Scene 2

*Alice Ford and Meg Page, two of the wives of Windsor, have become outraged
by their receipt of a most extraordinary letter from Sir John Falstaff:
each letter contains a declaration of Falstaff's passionate love for each of the ladies.*

*The two letters were written by the same hand, and by the same person:
they are identical, line for line, word for word.*

*These Windsor wives ar extemely determined women, and not faint of heart;
they plan to avenge the knight's gross insult and assault upon their propriety.*

*Meanwhile, Bardolph, Pistol and Dr. Caius, have united to deflate the fat knight's
shenanigans, and have alerted Mr. Ford to impending danger.
Ford is by no means inclined to shrug off Falstaff's threats lightly,
and envisions himself bedecked with horns, the infamous symbol of cuckoldry.
And like his wife, he believes in avenging the insult.*

*Amid this hurly burly, a real romance has blossomed.
Nannetta, the Ford daughter, has found her passion in the ardent young Fenton.*

*The scene unfolds as Meg Page and Dame Quickly appear;
they meet Alice and her daughter Nannetta at the Ford house.*

Meg:
Alice.

Alice:
Meg.

Meg:
Nannetta.

Alice:
Escivo appunto.
Per ridere con te.
Buon dì, comare.

Quickly:
Dio vi doni allegria.
Botton di rosa!

Alice:
Giungi in buon punto.
M'accade un fatto da trasecolare.

Meg:
Anche a me.

Quickly:
Che?

Nannetta:
Che cosa?

Alice:
Narra il tuo caso.

Meg:
Narra il tuo.

Quickly:
Narra.

Alice:
Promessa di non ciarlar.

Meg:
Ti pare?

Quickly:
Oibò! Vi pare?

Meg:
Friend Alice!

Alice:
Meg.

Meg: *(to Nannetta)*
My pretty one.

Alice:
I was just stepping out
to share a laugh with you.
Good day, Dame Quickly.

Quickly:
May the Lord make you merry.
Sweet Anne, my rosebud.

Alice:
Excellent timing!
I have the most fantastic tale to tell you.

Meg:
So have I.

Quickly: *(speaking with Nannetta)*
What?

Nannetta:
You also?

Alice: *(to Meg)*
Dear, you go first.

Meg:
After you.

Quickly:
Tell us, tell us!

Alice:
But swear not to breathe a word.

Meg:
Me gossip?

Quickly:
Me talk? My goodness!

Alice:
Dunque: se m'acconciassi a entrar ne' rei
propositi del diavolo, sarei
promossa al grado di cavalleressa!

Meg:
Anch'io.

Alice:
Motteggi.

Meg:
Non più parole,
ché qui sciupiamo la luce del sole.
Ho una lettera.

Alice:
Anch'io. Leggi.

Meg:
Leggi.

Nannetta e Quickly:
Oh!

Meg:
«Fulgida Alice! amor t'offro»
Ma come? Che cosa dice?
Salvo che il nome la frase è uguale.

Alice:
«Fulgida Meg, amor t'offro»

Meg:
«amor bramo»

Alice:
Qua «Meg», là «Alice»

Meg:
È tal e quale:
«Non domandar perché, ma dimmi»

Alice:
«t'amo»
Pur non gli offersi cagion.

Alice:
To strike a shameless bargain with the
devil, my rank shall be upgraded
with the name of Lady.

Meg:
Mine also.

Alice:
You're joking!

Meg:
If proof be needed,
instead of talking, look at this!
I've a letter, indisputable evidence.

Alice:
I also. Read it.

Meg: *(exchanging letters)*
Read it.

Nannetta and Quickly:
Oh!

Meg:
"Radiant Alice! Love I offer."
Good heavens! A second copy!
But for the name, the words are the same.

Alice:
"Radiant Meg, love I offer."

Meg:
"Burning passion!"

Alice:
Here Meg, there Alice.

Meg:
Letter for letter.
"Ask not the reason why, say only."

Alice:
"I love you."
I never once led him on!

Meg:
Il nostro caso è pur strano.

Quickly:
Guardiam con flemma.

Meg:
Gli stessi versi.

Alice:
Lo stesso inchiostro.

Quickly:
La stessa mano.

Nannetta:
Lo stesso stemma.

Alice e Meg:
«Sei la gaia comare, il compar gaio
son io, e fra noi due facciamo il paio»

Alice:
Già.

Nannetta:
A lui, lei, te.

Quickly:
Un paio in tre.

Alice:
«Facciamo il paio in un amor ridente
di donna bella e d'uomo appariscente»

Meg:
A story stranger than fiction.

Quickly:
Proceed with caution.

Meg:
The same phrases.

Alice:
The same malarkey.

Quickly:
The same hand writing.

Nannetta:
Even the paper.

Alice e Meg:
"As a fun-loving couple, we can double our
pleasures. We are made for one another."

Alice:
So!

Nannetta:
He, she, you!

Quickly:
A pair of three.

Alice:
A pair united by the fierce passion of a
gorgeous lady and a gentle man."

Alice:
«e il viso tuo su me risplenderà
come una stella sull'immensità»

Alice:
"And your face will shine upon me
like a star shining in the entire the universe."

Tutte:
Ah! Ah! Ah! Ah! Ah! Ah!

All:
Ha ha ha ha ha!

Alice:
«Rispondi al tuo scudiere,
John Falstaff cavaliere»

Alice:
"From one who loves you dearly,
John Falstaff, yours sincerely."

Tutte:
Mostro!

All:
Monster! Monster! Monster! Monster!

Alice:
Dobbiam gabbarlo.

Alice:
We'll make him tremble.

Nannetta:
E farne chiasso.

Nannetta:
And then display him like a clown.

Alice:
E metterlo in burletta.

Alice:
It's high time we teach him better.

Nannetta:
Oh! Oh! che spasso!

Nannetta:
What an uproar, what mayhem!

Quickly:
Che allegria!

Quickly:
What pleasure!

Meg:
Che vendetta!

Alice:
Ah, revenge!

Alice, Meg, Quickly, Nannetta, simultaneously.

A quell'otre, quel tino!
Quel re delle pance,
ci ha ancora le ciance
del bel vagheggino.

The tankard, the barrel!
His heyday is over
as a dashing young lover
in purple apparel.

E l'olio gli sgocciola
dall'adipe unticcio
e ancor ei ne snocciola
la strofa e il bisticcio!
Lasciam ch'ei le pronte
sue ciarle ne spifferi;
farà come i pifferi
che sceser dal monte.
Vedrai che se abbindolo quel grosso compar,
più lesto d'un guindolo lo faccio girar.

A flounder, a whopper!
A would-be wife-swapper,
a whale of a fellow,
professedly smitten,
cast up from the ocean
to land in Great Britain.
The vengeance now plotted
I'm in on the party,
a promise of laughter,
triumphant and hearty.

Quell'uom è un cannone,
se scoppia, ci spaccia.
Colui, se l'abbraccia,
ti schiaccia Giunone.
Vedrai che a un tuo cenno
quel mostro si spappola
e perde il suo senno
e corre alla trappola.
Potenza d'un fragile
sorriso di donna!
Scïenza d'un'agile
movenza di gonna!
Se il vischio lo impegola
lo udremo strillar.
E allor la sua fregola
vedremo svampar.

Se ordisci una burla,
vo' anch'io la mia parte.
Conviene condurla
con senno e con arte.
L'agguato ov'ei sdrucciola
convien ch'ei non scerna.
Già prese una lucciola
per una lanterna.
Perciò non dubito
che il gioco rïesca.
Bisogna offrir l'esca,
poi coglierlo subito.
E se i scillinguagnoli
sapremo adoprar,
vedremo a rigagnoli
quell'orco sudar.

Un flutto in tempesta
gittò sulla rena
di Windsor codesta
vorace balena.
Ma qui non ha spazio
da farsi più pingue;
ne fecer già strazio
le vostre tre lingue.
Tre lingue più allegre
d'un trillo di nacchere,
che spargon più chiacchiere
di sei cingallegre.

A whale of a fellow,
apparently smitten,
cast up from the ocean
to land in Great Britain.
A flounder, a whopper,
as I know and you know.
A would-be wife-swapper,
a challenge to Juno.
A man of immensity,
a mass of molasses,
he has a propensity
for rude and lewd passes.
Besides eccentricity,
he's laden with vices,
but for his duplicity
he's headed for crisis.

Despite his pomposity
he's bloated with gases
that make this monstrosity
king among asses.
As he swaggers boldly
his ardor increases,
but wait till our daggers
have ripped him to pieces.
The rogue will come wooing.
Though adept at rascality,
his agile mentality
will prove his undoing.
We women are wily,
and we are armed;
we'll test him
at ducking and dodging.

We'll drive him to insanity
by stoking his vanity,
our dexterity will foil insincerity.
The man will be vexed to see
the cards that I deal.
His head, will spin like a wheel
not from ecstasy,
I say in all modesty
we'll humble the heel.
Subdued, homeward bound he will steal.
So smothered in fantasy,
he'll come when we call.

Tal sempre s'esilari
quel bel cinguettar.
Così soglion l'ilari
comari ciarlar.

and we'll see how far he can fall.
We ladies move warily
with eyes on the ball.
And then we stand seven feet tall.

After the ladies depart, five men enter: Mr. Ford, Dr. Cajus, Fenton, Bardolfo, Pistola.
All cluster around Mr. Ford, and whisper to him simultaneously.

Dr. Cajus:
È un ribaldo, un furbo, un ladro,
un furfante, un turco, un vandalo;
l'altro dì mandò a soqquadro
la mia casa e fu uno scandalo.
Se un processo oggi gl'intavolo
sconterà le sue rapine.
Ma la sua più degna fine
sia d'andare in man del diavolo.
E quei due che avete accanto
gente sono di sua tribù,
non son due stinchi di santo
né due fiori di virtù.

Dr. Caius: *(to Ford)*
He's a thief, a thug, a vandal,
a repugnant slug, a rabid rat.
His behavior reeks of scandal;
he invaded my own residence.
A revolting dolt, and furthermore,
for deceiving, bragging, boasting,
I would gladly leave him roasting
over fires of hell forevermore.
With these rascals I'm also acquainted.
What a lot! A motley crew!
No, sir, not exactly sainted,
both are knaves and rascals, too.

Bardolfo:
Falstaff, sì ripeto, giuro,
(per mia bocca il ciel v'illumina)
contro voi, John Falstaff rumina
un progetto alquanto impuro.
Son uom d'arme e quell'infame
più non vo' che v'impozzangheri.
Non vorrei, no, escir dai gangheri
dell'onor per un reame!
Messer Ford, l'uomo avvisato
non è salvo che a metà.
Tocca a voi d'ordir l'agguato
che l'agguato stornerà.

Bardolph: *(to Ford)*
About Falstaff, sir, pay attention.
(I repeat, pay close attention.)
He is dabbling in skullduggery
of concern to you, unluckily.
A misdeed too dark to mention.
I'm a soldier, plain, outspoken,
never known to lie or fabricate,
and I'm not the man to abdicate
when a code of honor's broken.
Mister Ford, I've told my story,
on your mettle, rise to glory!
Give the dirty dog his due.

Ford:
(Un ronzio di vespe e d'avidi
calabron brontolamento,
un rombar di nembi gravidi
d'uragani è quel ch'io sento.
Il cerèbro un ebro allucina
turbamento di paura,
ciò che intorno a me si buccina,
è un sussurro di congiura.
Parlan quattro e uno ascolta;
qual dei quattro ascolterò?)

Ford:
(A buzz of wasps and greedy
calabron grunting,
a rogue of unmarried nuns,
and hurricanes is what I feel.
I'm looking like a drunk
disturbed by fear.
What surrounds me,
is a whisper of conspiracy.
Let four speak and one listen;
which of the four will I listen?)

Se parlaste uno alla volta
forse allor v'intenderò

If you speak one at a time
maybe I will understand you

Pistola:
Sir John Falstaff già v'appresta,
messer Ford, un gran pericolo.
Già vi pende sulla testa
qualche cosa a perpendicolo.

Messer Ford, fui già un armigero
di quell'uom dall'ampia cute;
or mi pento e mi morigero
per ragioni di salute.
La minaccia or v'è scoperta,
or v'è noto il ciurmador.
State all'erta, all'erta, all'erta!
Qui si tratta dell'onor.

Fenton:
Se volete io non mi perito
di ridurlo alla ragione
co' le brusche o co' le buone,
e pagarlo al par del merito.
Mi dà il cuore e mi solletica
(e sarà una giostra gaia)
di sfondar quella ventraia
iperbolicoapoplettica.
Col consiglio o co' la spada
se lo trovo al tu per tu,
o lui va per la sua strada
o lo assegno a Belzebù.

Ford:
Ripeti.

Pistola:
In due parole:
l'enorme Falstaff vuole
entrar nel vostro tetto,
beccarvi la consorte,
sfondar la cassaforte
e sconquassarvi il letto.

Dr. Cajus:
Caspita!

Ford:
Quanti guai!

Bardolfo:
Già le scrisse un biglietto...

Pistol: *(to Ford)*
He has planned a fate too horrid.
Yes indeed, and for you, sir, in particular.
I foresee upon your forehead
something standing perpendicular.

Mister Ford, be my confessional:
on that scoundrel I attended,
and rendered professional services,
praise the Lord, I've mended my ways!
Further shame can be averted
and you know what must be done.
Heed a warning, stand alerted!
Better yet, go get a gun.

Fenton: *(to Ford)*
If you wish, I hereby volunteer
to restore this man to reason;
either brain or brawn will season
the conniving, thriving cavalier.
Though I sniff a scent of a storm ahead,
it will give me special pleasure
taking on this monster's measure,
his dimensions so magnificent.
With a show of manly muscle,
if persuasion doesn't do,
I shall toss him in a tussle
from Peru to Timbuktu.

Ford: *(to Pistol)*
Say that again.

Pistol: *(to Ford)*
To put it briefly,
old Falstaff's plan is primarily
to sneak into your house,
and there seduce your spouse.
Though he hovers around your gold,
he'll first plough beneath your covers.

Dr. Caius:
Mercy!

Ford:
I'm finished!

Bardolph: *(to Ford)*
And a note, oh so tender.....

Pistola:
Ma quel messaggio abbietto
ricusai.

Pistol:
Through *me* he tried to send it to her.
No, I said!

Bardolfo:
Ricusai.

Bardolph:
As I did!

Pistola:
Badate a voi!

Pistol:
But stay on guard.

Bardolfo:
Badate!

Bardolph:
Oh, women!

Pistola:
Falstaff le occhieggia tutte,
che siano belle o brutte,
pulzelle o maritate.

Pistol:
All fit upon his platter,
dull, witty, plain or pretty,
single or wed, no matter.

Bardolfo:
La corona che adorna
d'Atteòn l'irte chiome
su voi già spunta.

Bardolph:
Sir, the crown husbands fear
upon your brow would appear
to already be sprouting.

Ford:
Come sarebbe a dir?

Ford:
What are you implying?

Bardolfo:
«Le corna»

Bardolph:
The horns!

Ford:
Brutta parola!

Ford:
Worst of all curses!

Dr. Cajus:
Ha voglie voraci il cavaliere.

Dr. Caius:
The knight has a keen, wandering eye.

Ford:
Sorveglierò la moglie.
Sorveglierò il messere.
Salvar vo' i beni miei
dagli appetiti altrui.

Ford:
My all too trusted wife
I'll hold in check for life,
Guarding what is mine by rights
from greedy appetites.

The four women reappear.

Fenton:
(È lei.)

Fenton: *(seeing Anne)*
(It's her.)

Nannetta:
(È lui.)

Nannetta: *(seeing Fenton)*
It's him!

Ford:
(È lei.)

Ford: *(seeing Alice)*
Herself!

Alice:
È lui.

Alice: *(seeing Ford)*
Himself!

Dr. Cajus:
È lei.

Dr. Caius: *(pointing to Alice)*
Herself!

Meg:
È lui.

Meg: *(indicating Ford)*
Himself!

Alice:
(S'egli sapesse!)

Alice:
(Slightly suspicious!)

Nannetta:
Guai!

Nannetta:
Careful!

Alice:
Schiviamo i passi suoi.

Alice:
The less he knows the better.

Ford, Dr. Caius, Bardolph and Pistol depart.

Meg:
Ford è geloso?

Meg:
Your husband's jealous?

Alice:
Assai.

Alice:
Insanely.

Quickly:
Zitto.

Nannetta:
Quiet!

Alice:
(Badiamo a noi.)

Alice:
(We'll slip away.)

Alice, Meg and Quickly depart, leaving Nannetta and Fenton alone.

Fenton:
Pst, pst, Nannetta.

Fenton:
Pst, Ann! My darling! Come here!

Nannetta:
Sss.

Nannetta:
Careful! For what?

Fenton:
Vien qua.

Fenton:
Two kisses.

Nannetta:
Taci. Che vuoi?

Nannetta:
Quiet. What do you want?

Fenton:
Due baci.

Nannetta:
In fretta.

Fenton:
In fretta.

Fenton:
I'll do so!

Nannetta:
Burning like embers,

Fenton:
Scented with flowers,

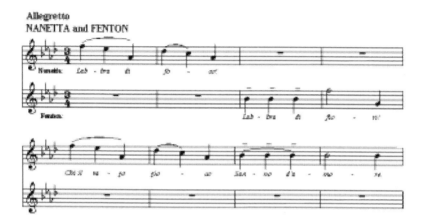

Nannetta e Fenton:
Labbra di foco! Labbra di fiore!

Nannetta:
Che il vago gioco sanno d'amore.

Fenton:
Che spargon ciarle,
che mostran perle,
belle a vederle, dolci a baciarle!
Labbra leggiadre!

Nannetta:
Man malandrine!

Fenton:
Ciglia assassine!
Pupille ladre!
T'amo!

Nannetta:
Imprudente.

Nannetta and Fenton:
Lips offering sun after showers.

Nannetta:
The vague game of love.

Fenton:
Sparkling and pearly,
trading in whispers,
love long remembers.
Lips soft and tender!

Nannetta:
Hands too aggressive!

Fenton:
Eyes that say yes, if
the heart surrenders.
I love you!

Nannetta:
Too impatient. No!

Fenton:
Sì, due baci.

Fenton:
Just another!

Nannetta:
Basta.

Nannetta:
Enough!

Fenton:
Mi piaci tanto!

Fenton:
What could be sweeter?

Nannetta:
Vien gente.

Nannetta:
Intruders!

Fenton:
Bocca baciata non perde ventura.

Fenton:
Lips that are kissed stay enchanted forever.

Nannetta:
Anzi rinnova come fa la luna.

Nannetta:
Kisses to the moon, ever reborn in splendor.

As the other women reappear, Fenton hides in the shrubbery.
Nannetta continues his song as she approaches the other women.

Alice:
Falstaff m'ha canzonata.

Alice:
Falstaff has tried to trick us.

Meg:
Merita un gran castigo.

Meg:
And he deserves no mercy.

Alice:
Se gli scrivessi un rigo?

Alice:
What if I send him a letter? Yes.

Nannetta:
Val meglio un'ambasciata.

Nannetta:
By messenger is best, Yes.

Alice:
Da quel brigante
tu andrai. Lo adeschi all'offa
d'un ritrovo galante con me.

Alice: *(to Quickly)*
The perfect person is you.
You can lure him toward me by proposing
a sweet rendezvous.

Quickly:
Questa è gaglioffa!

Quickly:
I shall die laughing!

Nannetta:
Che bella burla!

Nannetta:
How taunting!

Alice:
Prima, per attirarlo a noi, lo lusinghiamo, e
poi gliele cantiamo in rima.

Alice:
First, to disarm the man
we'll pour on the flattery.

The women resume singing fragments of their previous verses. The men leave.

Alice:
Qui più non si vagoli.

Alice:
No more of this dithering.

Nannetta:
Tu corri all'ufficio tuo.

Nannetta: *(to Quickly)*
You know what you have to do.

Alice:
Vo' ch'egli miagoli
d'amor come un micio.
È intesa?

Alice:
I want him yowling like a cat in the
moonlight.
You follow?

Quickly:
Sì.

Quickly:
Yes.

Nannetta:
È detta.

Nannetta:
All settled?

Alice:
Domani.

Alice:
Tomorrow.

Quickly:
Sì. Sì.

Quickly:
Yes, yes.

Alice:
Buon dì, Meg.

Alice:
Good day, Meg.

Quickly:
Nannetta, buon dì.

Quickly:
Good day to my Nannetta.

Nannetta:
Addio.

Nannetta:
Farewell.

Meg:
Buon dì.

Meg:
Good day.

Alice:
Vedrai che quell'epa terribile e tronfia
si gonfia.

Alice: *(to Meg)*
We'll see that big belly,
that paunch now so portly.

Alice, Meg, Quickly, Nannetta:
Si gonfia.e poi crepa.

Alice, Meg, Quickly, Nannetta:
It will expand and then go pop!

All exit laughing

END of ACT I

Act II — Scene I
At the Garter Inn.

Bardolph and Pistol have apparently recovered from their brief attack of virtue.
Falstaff is about to receive two visitors.
First, Dame Quickly will deliver Alice Ford's response to Falstaff's passionate invitation:
an unsubtle hint that her husband will be out of the house,
daily heading off for hunting, between 2:00 PM and 3:00 PM.

Falstaff's second visitor is Ford himself, incognito.
He pretends to be Mr. Brooke, and he is new to Windsor. He makes an outlandish offer
to Falstaff that few men could resist. Ford cleverly sets a trap for Falstaff;
but he will unwittingly walk into his own trap.

Bardolfo e Pistola:
Siam pentiti e contriti!

Bardolph and Pistol: *(beating their breasts)*
We repent, and we're contrite!

Molto piu lento
BARDOLFO and PISTOLA

Siam pen - ti - ti e con-tri - ti.

Falstaff:
L'uomo ritorna al vizio,
la gatta al lardo.

Falstaff:
Sinners return to vice
like mice to the larder.

Bardolfo e Pistola:
E noi, torniamo al tuo servizio.

Bardolph and Pistol:
Oh, if we could only serve you again!

Bardolfo:
Padron, là c'è una donna che alla vostra
presenza chiede d'essere ammessa.

Bardolph:
Oh, sir! A lady waits outside, requesting to
see you. Shall we ask her to enter?

Falstaff:
S'inoltri.

Falstaff:
My pleasure!

Quickly:
Reverenza!

Quickly: *(bowing deeply)*
Your reverence!

Assai moderato
DAME QUICKLY

Re-ver - ren - za!

Falstaff:
Buon giorno, buona donna.

Quickly:
Se vostra grazia vuole,
vorrei, segretamente, dirle quattro parole.

Falstaff:
T'accordo udienza.

Quickly:
Reverenza!
Madonna Alice Ford.

Falstaff:
Ebben?

Quickly:
Ahimè! Povera donna!
Siete un gran seduttore!

Falstaff:
Lo so. Continua.

Quickly:
Alice sta in gran agitazione d'amor per voi;
vi dice ch'ebbe la vostra lettera, che vi
ringrazia e che
suo marito esce sempre dalle due alle tre.

Falstaff:
Dalle due alle tre.

Falstaff:
Good day, my worthy woman.

Quickly:
Indulgent, sir, and lenient,
grant me some words alone and in private.

Falstaff: *(to Bardolph and Pistol)*
Allow us.

Quickly:
Save your reverence!
I come from Mistress Ford.

Falstaff: *(overly eager)*
Indeed?

Quickly:
Alas! She's an unhappy woman!
You're an acclaimed seducer!

Falstaff:
I know. Continue.

Quickly:
Alice is in great agitation: head over heels in
love with you. While tenderly kissing your
letter, she mentioned that her husband goes
hunting daily, at two to three.

Falstaff:
Leaves daily between two and three.

Quickly:
Vostra grazia a quell'ora
potrà liberamente salir ove dimora
la bella Alice! Povera donna! le angosce sue
son crudeli! ha un marito geloso!

Quickly:
He'll be gone for at least an hour when
you'll be free to enter. She will be waiting.
Unhappy woman! The cruel agonies she
suffers with such a jealous husband!

Falstaff:
Dalle due alle tre.
Le dirai che impazïente aspetto
quell'ora. Al mio dovere non mancherò.

Quickly:
Ben detto. Ma c'è un'altra ambasciata per
vostra grazia.

Falstaff:
Parla.

Quickly:
La bella Meg
(un angelo che innamora a guardarla)
anch'essa vi saluta molto amorosamente;
dice che suo marito è assai di rado assente.
Povera donna! un giglio di candore e di fé!
Voi le stregate tutte.

Falstaff:
Stregoneria non c'è,
ma un certo qual mio fascino personal.
Dimmi: l'altra sa di quest'altra?

Quickly:
Oibò! La donna nasce scaltra.
Non temete.

Falstaff:
Or ti vo' remunerar.

Quickly:
Chi semina grazie, raccoglie amore.

Falstaff:
Prendi, Mercuriofemina.

Quickly:
M'inchino.

Falstaff:
Alice è mia!

Falstaff:
Leaving daily at two to three.
Tell the lady I'll be counting the hours
until that blissful rendezvous.

Quickly:
So virile! Humor me again, I beg,
for I've one more message.

Falstaff:
Have you?

Quickly:
From lovely Meg,
(an angel, another heart you have broken),
sends an urgent message full of unspoken
desire, pained that her husband stays at
home and leaves rarely. Unhappy woman!
A flower pining to be bewitched!

Falstaff:
I claim no witching powers, I claim,
I'm certain, I confess, I don't know.
Tell me! Does either know the other?

Quickly:
Good Lord! Are women born so foolish?
Never fear it.

Falstaff:
Kindly take this small reward.

Quickly:
To sow seeds of love is reward enough.

Falstaff:
Cupid's winged carrier! Greet the ladies.

Quickly: *(before bowing and leaving)*
Your servant.

Falstaff:
Alice is mine!

Va', vecchio John, va', va' per la tua via.
Questa tua vecchia carne ancora spreme
qualche dolcezza a te.
Tutte le donne ammutinate insieme
si dannano per me!
Buon corpo di sir John, ch'io nutro e sazio,
va', ti ringrazio.

Well, gallant knight, onward to your glory!
This old but sturdy body can yet still
manage to stir the sleeping fire.
Women all over race to their ruin,
bedazzled by desire.
How grand to be Sir John, so well nourished!
Thus I have flourished!

Bardolfo:
Padron, di là c'è un certo messer mastro
Fontana che anela di conoscervi; offre una
damigiana di Cipro per l'asciolvere di vostra
signoria.

Bardolph:
Sir John! A certain Mister Brooke desires
your company. Although he doesn't know
you, he invites you, sir, to breakfast,
with a choice wine of Cyprus.

Falstaff:
Il suo nome è Fontana?

Falstaff:
Mister Brooke understands me.

Bardolfo:
Sì.

Bardolph:
Yes.

Falstaff:
Bene accolta sia
la fontana che spande un simile liquore!
Entri.

Falstaff:
Any river, stream or brook that flows with
well-fermented wine is welcome.
Bring him in.

Va', vecchio John, per la tua via!

So, gallant knight, onward to glory!

Ford, disguised, is preceded by Bardolph and Pistol.

Ford:
Signore, v'assista il cielo!

Ford:
Oh, sir! May heaven bless you!

Falstaff:
Assista voi pur, signore.

Falstaff:
I wish the same for you, sir.

Ford:
Io sono, davver, molto indiscreto, e vi
chiedo perdono, se,
senza cerimonie,
qui vengo e sprovveduto
di più lunghi preamboli.

Ford: *(respectful, reserved)*
I'm simply a plain, reserved fellow,
loath to bow, scrape and pander,
so do forgive my candor
in coming to the point
without beating about the bush.

Falstaff:
Voi siete il benvenuto.

Falstaff:
I welcome your frank approach.

Ford:
In me vedete un uomo ch'ha un'abbondanza
grande degli agi della vita; un uom che
spende e spande come più gli talenta pur di
passar mattana. Io mi chiamo Fontana!

Ford:
The Lord showered me with treasure,
which I spend at my pleasure.
Call me Brooke,
new to Windsor!

Falstaff: **Falstaff:** *(with the utmost cordiality)*

Caro signor Fontana!	Dear Mister Brooke, from the start
Voglio fare con voi più ampia conoscenza.	you've made an excellent impression.

Ford:
Caro sir John, desidero parlarvi in confidenza.

Ford:
Worthy Sir John,
then may I count on absolute discretion?

Bardolfo:
Attento!

Bardolph:
Attention!

Pistola:
Zitto!

Pistol:
Softer!

Bardolfo:
Guarda! Scommetto! Egli va dritto nel trabocchetto.

Bardolph:
Watch him! And wait! See the old flounder snap at the bait.

Pistola:
Ford se lo intrappola.

Pistol:
Ford will confuse him.

Bardolfo:
Zitto!

Both:
Softer!

Falstaff:
Che fate là?
V'ascolto.

Falstaff: *(loudly)*
Are you still here?
Go on, sir.

Ford:
Sir John, m'infonde ardire
un ben noto proverbio popolar: si suol dire
che l'oro apre ogni porta, che l'oro è un
talismano, che l'oro vince tutto.

Ford:
Sir John, I dare refer to a time-honored
cliché too often told: When the key is off all
doors will fly open.
To shining gold, one and all surrender.

Falstaff:
L'oro è un buon capitano
che marcia avanti.

Falstaff:
Gold is king of the mountain.
The conquering hero.

Ford:
Ebbene. Ho un sacco di monete
qua, che mi pesa assai.
Sir John, se voi volete
aiutarmi a portarlo.

Falstaff:
Con gran piacer, non so,
davver, per qual mio merito, messer.

Ford:
Ve lo dirò.
C,è a Windsor, una dama, bella e leggiadra
molto.
Si chiama Alice; è moglie di un certo Ford.

Falstaff:
V'ascolto.

Ford:
Io l'amo e lei non m'ama; le scrivo, non
risponde;
la guardo, non mi guarda; la cerco e si
nasconde.
Per lei sprecai tesori, gittai doni su doni,
escogitai, tremando, il vol delle occasioni.
Ahimè! tutto fu vano! Rimasi sulle scale,
negletto, a bocca asciutta, cantando un
madrigale.

Falstaff:
L'amor, l'amor che non ci dà mai tregue
finché la vita strugge
è come l'ombra.

Ford:
...che chi fugge...

Falstaff:
...insegue...

Ford:
...e chi l'insegue...

Falstaff:
...fugge...

Ford:
It happens the sack of gold I carry
weighs far too much for me.
Sir John, would you be kind enough
to share the burden?

Falstaff:
No need to ask! But why, my friend,
have I been chosen for the honor?

Ford:
Let me explain:
In Windsor lives a lady, lovely and oh so
charming!
Her name is Alice, and married to Ford.

Falstaff:
Poor lady!

Ford:
I love her, she's noncommittal.
She dismisses my letter.
My fervor matters little.
I plead, but still no kisses.
The gold I've spent, though vital,
I've sorrowfully squandered.
In vain! My passion is barely noted,
rejected, yet still devoted,
I sadly serenade her.

Falstaff:
"Oh, love! Oh, love! Though we ever adore
you, and mercifully implore you,
you are like a shadow."

Ford:
If it tries to leave you...

Falstaff:
...you follow...

Ford:
...tries to hold you...

Falstaff:
...you flee...

Ford e Falstaff:
...l'amor, l'amor!

Ford:
E questo madrigale l'ho appreso a prezzo d'or.

Falstaff:
Quest'è il destin fatale del misero amator.
Essa non vi diè mai luogo a lusinghe?

Ford:
No.

Falstaff:
Ma infin, perché v'aprite a me?

Ford:
Ve lo dirò:
voi siete un gentiluomo prode, arguto,
facondo, voi siete un uom di guerra,
voi siete un uom di mondo.

Falstaff:
Oh!

Ford:
Non vi adulo, e quello è un sacco di monete:
spendetele! spendetele! sì, spendete e spandete
tutto il mio patrimonio! Siate ricco e felice!
Ma, in contraccambio, chiedo che conquistiate Alice!

Falstaff:
Strana ingiunzion!

Ford:
Mi spiego: quella crudel beltà
sempre è vissuta in grande fede di castità.
La sua virtù importuna m'abbarbagliava gli occhi, la bella inespugnabile dicea:
«Guai se mi tocchi!»
Ma se voi l'espugnate, poi, posso anch'io sperar:
da fallo nasce fallo e allor. Che ve ne par?

Ford and Falstaff:
"Oh, love! Oh, love! Oh, love!"

Ford:
I paid a heavy price to learn this song of sorrow.

Falstaff:
The fatal destiny of a miserable amateur.
Did she never give you reason for hoping?

Ford:
No.

Falstaff:
Too bad, but why confide in me?

Ford:
Let me explain:
You have brawn and brilliance, decision,
and daring. A knight of noble bearing,
a man above the millions.

Falstaff: *(with a gesture of modesty)*
Oh?

Ford:
I'll not flatter. A man like you needs lots of money, So take the stuff.
If not enough, come for more.
Scatter my entire fortune to the winds.
But on one condition:
you will seduce sweet Alice!

Falstaff:
I don't get it.

Ford:
Quite simple:
She's proper as well as proud,
and waves a banner,
"Sir, keep your distance!"
I'm met with stern resistance.
Make her fall, and clear the way for me.
The wall then has to crumble.
So? What do you say?

Falstaff:
Prima di tutto, senza complimenti, messere,
accetto il sacco. E poi (fede di cavaliere:
qua la mano!) farò le vostre brame sazie.
Voi, la moglie di Ford possederete.

Ford:
Grazie!

Falstaff:
Io son già molto innanzi
(non c'è ragion ch'io taccia
con voi): fra una mezz'ora sarà nelle mie
braccia.

Ford:
Chi?

Falstaff:
Alice. Essa mandò dianzi una, confidente
per dirmi che quel tanghero di suo marito è
assente
dalle due alle tre.

Ford:
Lo conoscete?

Falstaff:
Il diavolo
se lo porti all'inferno con Menelao suo
avolo!
Vedrai! Te lo cornifico netto! se mi frastorna
gli sparo una girandola di botte sulle corna!
Quel messer Ford è un bue! Un bue!
Te lo corbello, vedrai!
Ma è tardi. Aspettami qua.
Vado a farmi bello.

Ford:
È sogno o realtà? Due rami enormi
crescon sulla mia testa.
È un sogno? Mastro Ford! Mastro Ford!
Dormi?
Svegliati! Su! Ti desta!
Tua moglie sgarra e mette in mal assetto
l'onore tuo, la tua casa ed il tuo letto!

Falstaff:
Waste no words, no ifs, no buts.
I accept your gold. I'll serve you well.
That task is well within my power:
the fair Mistress Ford will knuckle under.

Ford:
Bravo!

Falstaff:
I'm far along already.
(No need to hide my secret from him.)
In half an hour
I plan to enjoy the lady.

Ford:
Who?

Falstaff:
Dear Alice, sent me a message,
to inform me that the fool she calls a
husband goes hunting,
leaving daily between two and three.

Ford:
You know that?

Falstaff:
Let him go to the devil,
damned by his own stupidity.
So gullible!
That knucklehead!
Today, we'll see him cuckolded
fairly, squarely.
He's a blundering moron.
Be patient. I shall soon return.
I'm off to make myself handsome.

Ford:
A nightmare? Or is it real?
Two horns have sprouted on my forehead.
A dream, no?
Mister Ford! Mister Ford! Sleeping?
On your toes! Rise! Awaken!
Your wife corrupted, her vows invalidated,
and your bed and your honor contaminated!

L'ora è fissata, tramato l'inganno;	Messages bandied, swindled and cheated.
sei gabbato e truffato!	And all over town,
E poi diranno	they tell us that a jealous man
che un marito geloso è un insensato!	is demented.
Già dietro a me nomi d'infame conio	Scorn and disdain, the knowing smile,
fischian passando; mormora lo scherno.	idle banter, sly insinuation.

O matrimonio, inferno!	Infernal marriage! Why did I marry?
Donna: demonio!	Women! Demons!
Nella lor moglie abbian fede i babbei!	Only a fool blindly trusts them.
Affiderei la mia birra a un tedesco,	I'd sooner trust my beer to a German,
tutto il mio desco a un olandese lurco,	or a bone before a starving spaniel,
la mia bottiglia d'acquavite a un turco,	or stake my life upon a lottery
non mia moglie a sé stessa.	than trust a wife left alone.
O laida sorte!	A grim reprisal!
Quella brutta parola in cor mi torna:	That brutal word shall taunt me:
«Le corna!» Bue! Capron! le fusa torte!	"You cuckold!" Branded! Accursed!
Ah! «le corna! le corna!»	Ah! You cuckold! You cuckold!
Ma non mi sfuggirai! no! sozzo, reo,	Now let him fear the worst! Ah!
dannato epicureo!	Lecher! Glutton!
Prima li accoppio	Soon you crow and cackle!
e poi li colgo. Io scoppio!	First let them couple, then I shall tackle.
Vendicherò l'affronto!	I shall avenge the betrayal!
Laudata sempre sia	I shall forever praise
nel fondo del mio cor la gelosia.	that fever in my jealous heart.
Falstaff:	**Falstaff:** *(returning)*
Eccomi qua. Son pronto.	Here I am, dressed and ready.
M'accompagnate un tratto?	Do join me, my good fellow.
Ford:	**Ford:**
Vi metto sulla via.	You first and I shall follow.
Falstaff:	**Falstaff:**
Prima voi.	After you.
Ford:	**Ford:**
Prima voi.	After you.

Falstaff:
No, sono in casa mia.
Passate.

Falstaff:
No, no! You're my guest of honor.
Lead on, sir.

Ford:
Prego.

Ford:
You first.

Falstaff:
È tardi. L'appuntamento preme.

Falstaff:
It's late. We mustn't keep the lady waiting.

Ford:
Non fate complimenti.

Ford:
I bow unto my better.

Falstaff e Ford:
Ebben; passiamo insieme.

Falstaff and Ford:
The, we'll leave together.

They exit arm in arm.

Act II — Scene 2

At the Ford house, Alice awaits her rendezvous with Sir John Falstaff.
The Winders wives have carefully laid their plans: the rendezvous is to be interrupted
by Meg Page, who will burst in with the announcement that Mr. Ford,
breathing fire and thunder, is on the way. However, the plan does not include the
frantic appearance of Dame Quickly a few seconds later, with the staggering news
that Ford, has became a raging maniac, and is coming with shot gun in hand.

The revenge on Falstaff has gone much further than intended. Danger is imminent.
Falstaff must be concealed, then removed — a daunting challenge.

Another plot is brewing: for some undisclosed reason, Ford has decided
that his daughter Nannetta is to marry old Dr. Caius,
unaware that his daughter is in love with young Fenton.

Alice:
Presenteremo un bill, per una tassa
al parlamento, sulla gente grassa.

Alice:
It will be too bad for some if Parliament
taxes a person by tonnage.

Quickly:
Comari!

Quickly: *(at the door)*
Good neighbors!

Alice:
Ebben?

Alice:
You're back!

Meg:
Che c'è?

Meg:
What news?

Quickly:
Sarà sconfitto!

Quickly:
Prepare to conquer.

Alice:
Brava!

Alice:
Brava!

Quickly:
Fra poco gli farem la festa!

Quickly:
You'll soon have him round your finger.

Alice e Meg:
Bene!

Alice and Meg:
Well done.

Quickly:
Piombò nel laccio a capofitto.

Quickly:
He took the bait, hook, line and sinker.

Alice:
Narrami tutto, lesta.

Alice:
Tell us, tell us, from the beginning!

Meg:
Lesta.

Meg:
Tell us!

Quickly:
Giunta all'«Albergo della Giarrettiera»
chiedo d'essere ammessa alla presenza
del cavalier, segreta messaggera.
Sir John si degna d'accordarmi udienza,
m'accoglie tronfio in furfantesca posa:
«Buon giorno, buona donna.»

Quickly:
I arrived at the seedy, shady inn they call
The Garter, and asked to see the amorous
knight upon a private matter.
The great Sir John grants a meeting, and
then greets me with pomp and splendor:
"Good day, my worthy woman."

«Reverenza!»
A lui m'inchino molto ossequïosamente,
poi passo alle notizie ghiotte.
Lui beve grosso ed ogni mia massiccia
frottola inghiotte.
Infine, a farla spiccia,
vi crede entrambe innamorate cotte
delle bellezze sue.
E lo vedrete presto ai vostri piè.

Enough of your reverence!
I make a curtsey,
so very prim and proper!
Then soon we settle down to business.
He eagerly swallows the bait.
In short, he believes that you both
find him enthralling, and soon,
you will see him falling,
falling at your feet.

Alice:
Quando?

Alice:
When?

Quickly:
Oggi, qui, dalle due alle tre.

Quickly:
Today, two o'clock on the dot.

Alice:
Son già le due.
Olà! Ned Will!
Già tutto ho preparato.
Portate qui la cesta del bucato.

Quickly:
Sarà un affare gaio!

Alice:
Nannetta, e tu non ridi? Che cos'hai?
Tu piangi? Che cos'hai?
Dillo a tua madre.

Nannetta:
Mio padre...

Alice:
Ebben?

Nannetta:
Mio padre,
vuole ch'io mi mariti al Dottor Cajo!

Alice:
A quel pedante?

Quickly:
Oibò!

Meg:
A quel gonzo!

Alice:
A quel grullo!

Nannetta:
A quel bisavolo!

Alice, Meg, Quickly:
No! No!

Nannetta:
No! No! Piuttosto lapidata viva.

Alice:
Da una mitraglia di torsi di cavolo.

Alice:
It's two already.
Ola! Ned! Will!
My men are put on notice.
Bring the laundry basket with the washing.

Quickly:
Sir John will take a spill.

Alice:
My daughter, aren't you laughing.
Are you ill? So tearful!
What is wrong? Come, tell your mother.

Nannetta:
My father...

Alice:
Go on...

Nannetta:
My father says I'm to marry
that old Doctor Caius.

Alice:
That dusty fossil?

Quickly:
Oh, dear!

Meg:
That eccentric?

Alice:
That fanatic?

Nannetta:
That walking skeleton!

Alice, Meg, Quickly:
No! No!

Nannetta:
No! No! I'd sooner die by suffocation.

Alice:
Pelt me with turnips and cabbages.

Quickly:
Ben detto!

Meg:
Brava!

Alice:
Non temer.

Nannetta:
Evviva!
Col Dottor Cajo non mi sposerò!

Alice:
Mettete là. Poi, quando avrò chiamato,
vuoterete la cesta nel fossato.

Nannetta:
Bum!

Alice:
Taci.Andate.

Nannetta:
Che bombardamento!

Alice:
Prepariamo la scena. Qua una sedia.

Nannetta:
Qua il mio liuto.

Alice:
Apriamo il paravento.
Bravissime! Così. Più aperto ancora.
Fra poco s'incomincia la commedia.

Gaie comari di Windsor! è l'ora!
L'ora di alzar la risata sonora!
L'alta risata che scoppia, che scherza,
che sfolgora, armata di dardi e di sferza!

Gaie comari, festosa brigata!
Sul lieto viso
spunti il sorriso,
splenda del riso
l'acuto fulgor!

Quickly:
Me also!

Meg:
Brava!

Alice:
Have no fear!

Nannetta:
Hallelujah!
Then I'll just say no to the doctor!

Alice: *(to servants with the basket)*
Right over there. Then, when I give the
order, dump it into the river.

Nannetta:
Plop!

Alice: *(to servants who are leaving)*
Hush! Be ready.

Nannetta:
Pride will take a tumble.

Alice:
Let's prepare the scene. Here, the chair.

Nannetta:
There, my lute.

Alice:
We ought to open the screen.
Bravissimo! All set!
A little wider. Curtain up, the comedy begins.

You merry women of Windsor,
the time is ripe for laughter
that'll topple the swaggering braggart.
An arsenal with darts but no daggers.

Neighbors united!
Join the brigade of fun-loving mortals,
storming the portals of pomp and pride.
Be merry,
discreet or outrageous!

Favilla incendiaria
di gioia nell'aria,
di gioia nel cor.

A noi! Tu la parte farai che ti spetta.

Meg:
Tu corri il tuo rischio
col grosso compar.

Quickly:
Io sto alla vedetta.

Alice:
Se sbagli ti fischio.

Nannetta:
Io resto in disparte
sull'uscio a spiar.

Alice:
E mostreremo all'uomo che l'allegria
d'oneste donne ogni onestà comporta.
Fra le femmine quella è la più ria
che fa da gattamorta.

Quickly:
Eccolo! È lui!

Alice:
Dov'è?

Quickly:
Poco discosto.

Nannetta:
Presto.

Quickly:
A salir s'avvia.

Alice:
Tu di qua. Tu di là!

Nannetta:
Al posto!

The joy is contagious
and spreads far and wide,
so be alert and ready!

(to Meg)
You know what to do, and when to do it?

Meg: *(to Alice)*
You may come to rue it if the game goes
awry.

Quickly:
I'll stand on alert.

Alice: *(to Quickly)*
Be quick in case I whistle.

Nannetta:
I'll wait by the window
and spy and survey.

Alice:
To those that complain and object,
before you condemn a lady, consider
that the woman most prone to be severely
frowned upon, is likely the most shady.

Quickly:
On your mark! Get set!

Alice:
He's here?

Quickly:
Too close for comfort.

Nannetta:
Hurry!

Quickly:
He is on the stairway.

Alice:
Over here! Over there!

Nannetta:
On duty!

Falstaff:
Alfin t'ho colto,
raggiante fior, t'ho colto!
Ed or potrò morir felice.
Avrò vissuto molto
dopo quest'ora di beato amor.

Alice:
O soave sir John!

Falstaff:
Mia bella Alice!
Non so far lo svenevole,
né lusingar, né usar frase fiorita,
ma dirò tosto un mio pensier colpevole.

Alice:
Cioè?

Falstaff:
Cioè: vorrei che mastro Ford
passasse a miglior vita.

Alice:
Perché?

Falstaff:
Perché? Lo chiedi?
Saresti la mia lady
e Falstaff il tuo lord!

Alice:
Povera lady inver!

Falstaff:
Degna d'un re.
T'immagino fregiata del mio stemma,
mostrar fra gemma e gemma
la pompa del tuo sen.
Nell'iri ardente e mobile dei rai
dell'adamante,
col picciol piè nel nobile
cerchio d'un guardinfante
risplenderai!
Più fulgida d'un ampio arcobalen.

Falstaff: *(entering)*
At last to gather
my fragrant flower. My treasure!
Now I can die with a contented heart.
Why live a moment longer
after this hour in the arms of love?

Alice:
Oh, my tender Sir John!

Falstaff:
My lovely Alice!
Though my talents are minimal;
there is no man alive milder and sweeter.
Yet I confess to a highly criminal secret.

Alice:
My word!

Falstaff:
I wish that Mister Ford
might stand before St. Peter.

Alice:
But why?

Falstaff:
But why? You're asking?
Then you could be my Lady,
and I could be your Lord.

Alice:
A Lady unworthy of you!

Falstaff:
Worthy of a king!
My coat of arms, embellished by your
beauty, will glorify that bosom where all
my passions lie.
I expect to see your jeweled hand
in rare pearl and ruby splendor.
Your slippered foot — sheer ecstasy!
So delicate and slender.
Your divine eyes will far outshine
God's rainbows glowing on high.

Alice:
Ogni più bel gioiel mi nuoce e spregio
il finto idolo d'or.
Mi basta un vel legato in croce, un fregio
al cinto e in testa un fior.

Falstaff:
Sirena!

Alice:
Adulator!

Falstaff:
Soli noi siamo
e non temiamo agguato.

Alice:
Ebben?

Falstaff:
Io t'amo!

Alice:
Voi siete nel peccato!

Falstaff:
Sempre l'amor l'occasïone azzecca.

Alice:
Sir John!

Falstaff:
Chi segue vocazion non pecca.
T'amo! e non è mia colpa.

Alice:
Se tanta avete vulnerabil polpa.

Falstaff:

Alice:
Oh, lead me not unto temptation!
I've little need of gold, heaven knows,
and pay no heed to decoration.
Instead of fancy frills, just a simple rose.

Falstaff: *(trying to embrace her)*
Enchanting!

Alice: *(pulling away)*
You go too far.

Falstaff:
Alone together,
we need fear no intruders.

Alice:
You mean?

Falstaff:
I love you!

Alice:
You're prompted by the devil.

Falstaff:
True love must seize the rare occasion.

Alice:
Sir John!

Falstaff:
A sin to find my true vocation?
I pursue my passion, dazzled by you.

Alice:
Your flesh is weak, but seems all too solid.

Falstaff:

Quand'ero paggio
del duca di Norfolk ero sottile,
ero un miraggio
vago, leggero, gentile, gentile.

Quello era il tempo del mio verde aprile,
quello era il tempo del mio lieto maggio.
Tant'ero smilzo, flessibile e snello
che avrei guizzato attraverso un anello.

Alice:
Voi mi celiate. Io temo i vostri inganni.
Temo che amiate.

Falstaff:
Chi?

Alice:
Meg.

Falstaff:
Colei? M'è in uggia la sua faccia.

Alice:
Non traditemi, John...

Falstaff:
Mi par mill'anni
d'averti fra le braccia.
T'amo!

Alice:
Per carità!

Falstaff:
Vieni!

Quickly:
Signora Alice!

Falstaff:
Chi va là?

Quickly:
Signora Alice!

Alice:
Che c'è?

When I was the page, to the Duke of
Norfolk, I was trim as a sparrow.
quick on the mark, bright as a lark,
and swift as an arrow.

It was the springtime of all my glory!
Days full of love, fleet and transitory.
Then I was slender, nimble, thin enough to
slip through the eye of a needle.

Alice:
How charming, although I've heard a
different story about another woman!

Falstaff:
Who?

Alice:
Meg.

Falstaff:
That shrew! Her face would scare an ogre.

Alice:
Sir, don't play with me.

Falstaff:
I've waited a thousand years for this sweet
moment.
I love you!

Alice:
Do have a heart!

Falstaff:
Always!

Quickly: *(from outside)*
Good Mistress Alice!

Falstaff:
Who is that?

Quickly: *(agitated)*
Good Mistress Alice!

Alice:
What now?

Quickly:
Mia signora!
C'è mistress Meg, e vuol parlarvi, sbuffa,
strepita, s'abbaruffa.

Quickly: *(rushing in)*
Oh, my lady!
Our neighbor Meg! She said it's urgent!
Shaking, staggering, looking frantic!

Falstaff:
Alla malora!

Falstaff:
Speak of the devil.

Quickly:
E vuol passare e la trattengo a stento.

Quickly:
She demands to see you.

Falstaff:
Dove m'ascondo?

Falstaff:
Where can I hide?

Alice:
Dietro il paravento.

Alice:
Here behind the screen.

Falstaff hides behind the screen. Quickly departs. Meg rushes in, frightened.

Meg:
Alice! che spavento!
Che chiasso! Che discordia!
Non perdere un momento, fuggi!

Meg:
Friend Alice! Pandemonium!
Disaster! Rack and ruin!
You must not waste a second. Flee!

Alice:
Misericordia! Che avvenne?

Alice:
Oh, heaven help me! What's happened?

Meg:
Il tuo consorte vien gridando
«accorr'uomo!»

Meg:
Your husband's coming, and he's crying
and swearing, "Bloody murder!"

Alice:
Parla più forte.

Alice:
Speak even louder.

Meg:
Che vuol scannare un uomo!

Meg:
He'll slice the man to ribbons.

Alice:
Non ridere.

Alice:
Stop laughing so.

Meg:
Ei correva
invaso da tremendo
furor! Maledicendo
tutte le figlie d'Eva!

Meg:
He swears he'll storm the house.
He's stark raving mad,
and hurling curses
on all the daughters of Satan.

Alice:
Misericordia!

Alice:
Oh, Lord, have mercy!

Meg:
Dice che un tuo ganzo hai nascosto,
lo vuole ad ogni costo scoprir.

Quickly:
Signora Alice!
Vien mastro Ford! Salvatevi!
È come una tempesta!
Strepita, tuona, fulmina,
si dà dei pugni in testa,
scoppia in minacce ed urla.

Alice:
Dassenno oppur da burla?

Quickly:
Dassenno. Egli scavalca
le siepi del giardino,
lo segue una gran calca
di gente è già vicino.
Mentr'io vi parlo
ei valca l'ingresso.

Ford:
Malandrino!

Falstaff:
Il diavolo cavalca
sull'arco di un violino!

Meg:
He claims that you're concealing a lover:
a knave that he'll uncover and kill.

Quickly: *(returning, in great agitation)*
He's on the warpath! Your husband's here.
Go instantly! He's wilder than a tiger.
He's snarling, scowling, and sputtering,
acting like a savage,
and howling and hurling abuse.

Alice:
(I'd almost think you meant it.)

Quickly:
Believe it!
He made his way through the hedge around
the garden with half the men of Windsor.
There's a riot! An insurrection!
And as we speak, they're charging toward
the door.

Ford: *(from outside)*
Open, open!

Falstaff: *(listening from behind the screen)*
The devil ups the ante.
They've caught me in flagrante.

Ford bursts in, followed closely by Dr. Caius, Fenton, Bardolph and Pistol.

Ford:
Chiudete le porte! Sbarrate le scale!
Seguitemi a caccia! Scoviamo il cignale!

Correte sull'orme, sull'usta.

Tu fruga negli anditi.

Bardolfo e Pistola:
A caccia!

Ford:
Sventate la fuga!
Cercate là dentro!

Ford:
Bolt the doors! Surround the stairway!
We hounds and hunters will capture the quarry.

(to Doctor Caius)
Go sniff out the animal's traces.
(to Fenton)
You search every corridor.

Bardolph and Pistol:
To the hunt!

Ford:
Cut off his escape,
look upstairs in my chamber.

Alice:
Sei tu dissennato? Che fai?

Ford:
Chi c'è dentro quel cesto?

Alice:
Il bucato.

Ford:
Mi lavi! rea moglie!

Tu, piglia le chiavi,
rovista le casse, va'.
Ben tu mi lavi!
Al diavolo i cenci!
Sprangatemi l'uscio del parco!
Camice, gonnelle, or ti sguscio,
briccon! Strofinacci! Via! Via! Cuffie rotte!
Ti sguscio. Lenzuola, berretti da notte.
Non c'è.

Alice, Quickly, Meg:
Che uragano!

Ford:
Cerchiam sotto il letto.
Nel forno, nel pozzo, nel bagno, sul tetto,
in cantina.

Alice:
È farnetico!

Quickly:
Cogliam tempo.

Alice:
Troviamo modo com'egli fugga.

Meg:
Nel panier.

Alice:
No, là dentro non c'entra, è troppo grosso.

Falstaff:
Vediam; sì, c'entro, c'entro.

Alice: *(confronting Ford)*
Sir, have you gone crazy? Or what?

Ford:
Aha! What's in the basket?

Alice:
Tons of laundry.

Ford:
Then clean up your conscience!
(giving keys to Caius, who runs out)
Take over the keys
to the cupboards and closets.
(back to Alice) All your own doing!
(kick the basket) To hell with these tatters!
(calling out) Again, go search the garden.
Some towels, some collars, greasy napkins.
Smelly stockings.
More linen and bundles of bedding.
Not there.

Alice, Quickly, Meg:
Fire and thunder!

Ford:
Look under the tables. Go inside and
outside, The chimney, the attic and the
cellar.

Alice:
Sheer insanity!

Quickly:
Now's the moment!

Alice:
He must escape some way or other.

Meg:
With the wash!

Alice:
No, too big for the basket: far too hefty.

Falstaff: *(emerging)*
I'll try! Come! Help me! Help me!

Alice:
Corro a chiamare i servi.

Alice:
I'll go and call my servants.

Meg:
Sir John! Voi qui? Voi?

Meg: *(pretending surprise)*
Sir John! You here? Well!

Falstaff:
T'amo amo te sola.
salvami! salvami!

Falstaff:
Angel! My one beloved!
Save me now! Help me out!

Meg e Quickly:
Svelto! Lesto!

Meg and Quickly: *(to Falstaff)*
Tuck him in, tuck him in! Easy does it.

Falstaff:
Ahi! Ahi! Ci sto! Copritemi!

Falstaff:
Ahi! Ahi! I'm in! Now cover me.

Quickly:
Presto! colmiamo il cesto.

Quickly: *(to Meg)*
Lower! And hold your nose!

While the wives busily stuff Falstaff into the basket, Fenton and Anne enter.

Nannetta:
Vien qua!

Nannetta:
This way!

Fenton:
Che chiasso!

Fenton:
What fury!

Nannetta:
Quanti schiamazzi!
Segui il mio passo.

Nannetta:
Such a commotion!
Calling for caution.

Fenton:
Casa di pazzi!

Fenton:
People gone crazy.

Nannetta:
Qui ognun delira
con vario error.
Son pazzi d'ira

Nannetta:
Snapping and snarling,
shouting and shoving.
They burn with anger.

Fenton:
E noi d'amor.

Fenton:
We burn with love.

Nannetta:
Seguimi. Adagio.

Nannetta: *(with Fenton, behind the screen)*
Follow close, my darling.

Fenton:
Nessun m'ha scorto.

Fenton:
...and stay unseen.

Nannetta:
Tocchiamo il porto.

Nannetta:
Here we can linger.

Fenton:
Siamo a nostr'agio.

Fenton:
Saved by the screen.

Nannetta:
Sta' zitto e attento.

Nannetta:
Away from the action.

Fenton:
Vien sul mio petto!

Fenton: *(embracing her)*
In my protection.

Nannetta:.
Il paravento sia benedetto!

Nannetta: *(hiding behind the screen)*
Here is safe haven.

Dr. Cajus:
Al ladro!

Dr. Caius: *(shouting from outside)*
Keep searching!

Ford:
Al pagliardo!

Ford: *(also outside)*
Find the bounder!

Dr. Cajus:
Squartatelo!

Dr. Caius:
Draw and quarter him!

Ford:
Al ladro! C'è?

Ford: *(to Pistol)*
Surround him! Yes?

Pistola:
No.

Pistol:
No.

Ford:
C'è?

Ford: *(to Bardolph, appearing)*
Yes?

Bardolfo:
Non c'è, no.

Bardolph:
No luck. None.

Ford:
Vada a soqquadro la casa.

Ford:
Tear down the house if you have to.

Dr. Cajus:
Non trovo nessuno.

Dr. Caius:
He's not up the chimney.

Ford:
Eppur giuro che l'uomo è qua dentro. Ne
sono sicuro! sicuro! sicuro!

Ford:
He's certainly hiding here,
no question about it.

Dr. Cajus:
Sir John! Sarò gaio quel dì ch'io ti veda dar calci a rovaio!

Ford:
T'arrendi furfante! T'arrendi! O bombardo le mura!

Dr. Cajus:
T'arrendi!

Ford:
Vien fuora! Codardo! Sugliardo!

Bardolfo e Pistola:
Nessuno!

Ford:
Cercatelo ancora! T'arrendi! Scanfardo!

Dr. Cajus:
Vieni fuori! Non c'è!
Pappalardo! Beon! Bada a te!

Ford:
Scagnardo! Falsardo! Briccon!
C'è.

Dr. Cajus:
C'è.

Ford, Dr. Cajus, Bardolfo,Pistola:

Se t'agguanto!
Se ti piglio!
Se t'acciuffo!
Se t'acceffo!
Ti sconquasso!
T'arronciglio come un can!
Ti rompo il ceffo!

Dr. Cajus:
Guai a te!

Ford:
Prega il tuo santo!

Dr. Caius:
Sir John, I will dance the fandango the day that you hang, you rascal!

Ford:
Come out, you old lecher, or I'll leave nothing standing.

Dr. Caius:
Surrender!

Ford:
This time I'm challenging him!

Bardolph and Pistol: *(returning)*
Absconded!

Ford: *(to Bardolph and Pistol)*
Try harder, keep searching.

Dr. Caius:
Come out here! Not there! Bloated boozer, you souse, Oh, beware!

Ford: *(looking behind the screen)*
You boozer, bounder. I warn you, beware!
Ha!

Dr. Caius:
Ha!

Ford, Dr. Caius, Bardolph, Pistol:
(moving slowly toward the screen)
When I catch you!
When I nab you!
When I grab you!
When I snatch you!
I will crush you!
I will beat you black and blue!.
I'll bury your bones!

Dr. Caius:
On your knees!

Ford:
Pray to St. Mary.

Bardolfo:
Non si trova.

Pistola:
Non si coglie.

Ford:
L'ho trovato.
Là c'è Falstaff con mia moglie.

Bardolfo:
Sozzo can vituperato!

Ford, Pistola, Dr. Cajus:
Zitto!

Ford:
Urlerai dopo.
Là s'è udito il suon d'un bacio.

Bardolfo:
Noi dobbiam pigliare il topo
mentre sta rodendo il cacio.

Falstaff:
Son cotto!

Quickly e Meg:
Facciamo le viste
d'attendere ai panni;
pur ch'ei non c'inganni
con mosse impreviste.
Fin'or non s'accorse
di nulla, egli può
sorprenderci forse,
confonderci no.

Facciamogli siepe
fra tanto scompiglio.
Ne' giuochi il periglio
è un grano di pepe.
Il rischio è un diletto
che accresce 'ardor,
che stimola in petto
gli spirti e il cor.

Bardolph:
I don't find him

Pistol:
Not there.

Ford: *(indicating the screen)*
I have got him.
He's there, hiding with my wife.

Bardolph:
Oh, the dirty drunken mongrel!

Ford, Pistol, Dr. Caius:
Quiet, quiet, quiet!

Ford:
Quiet! Hold down the thunder.
I heard a kiss.

Bardolph:
We need to catch the mouse
while he's in the act.

Falstaff: *(from inside the basket)*
I'm stifling. I'm cooking.

Quickly and Meg:
Attend to the wash
and watch out for surprises;
Our labors are lost
if the basket capsizes.
The game has begun
so be bolder, be braver;
a small pinch of pepper
enhances the flavor.

No matter the pressure,
the risk is a pleasure
and part of the fun.
The trouble is triple:
a man with a gun
a wife in the middle,
a rogue on the run,
they enlighten the heart.

Falstaff:
Affogo!

Quickly:
Sta' sotto.

Meg:
Or questi s'insorge.

Quickly:
Se l'altro ti scorge sei morto.

Falstaff:
Son cotto!

Meg:
Sta' sotto!

Falstaff:
Che caldo!

Quickly:
Sta' sotto!

Falstaff:
Mi squaglio!

Ford:
Ragioniam. Colpo non vibro
senza un piano di battaglia.

Gli altri:
Bravo.

Dr. Cajus:
Un uom di quel calibro
con un soffio ci sbaraglia.

Nannetta e Fenton:
Mentre quei vecchi corron la giostra,
noi di sottecchi corriam la nostra.
L'amor non ode tuon né bufere,
vola alle sfere beate e gode.
Bella! Ridente!
Oh! come pieghi verso i miei prieghi
donnescamente!
L'attimo ancora cogliam che brilla,
è la scintilla viva dell'ora.

Falstaff:
I'm roasting.

Quickly:
Stay down.

Meg:
Be careful, stay under.

Quickly:
Be careful, you're dead if discovered.

Falstaff:
I'm cooked!

Meg:
Stay down!

Falstaff:
What do I hear!

Quickly:
Stay down!

Falstaff:
I'm being torn apart!

Ford:
Not so fast! For greater luster
we require a plan of battle.

Others:
Bravo, bravo!

Dr. Caius:
A man of bluff and bluster
can soon derange and rattle.

Nannetta and Fenton: *(behind the screen)*
The pain is over!
I gaze in wonder as you surrender
to your true lover.
I fell in love the moment we met,
and you were smiling because you knew.
While busy people bluster and blunder,
blinded by passion and torn asunder,
love does not hear the crashes of thunder;
floating in bliss, at peace, we gaze in wonder.

Come ti vidi m'innamorai,
e tu sorridi perché lo sai.
Lo spiritello d'amor volteggia.
Già un sogno bello d'imene albeggia.
Tutto delira, sospiro e riso.
Sorride il viso e il cor sospira.
Fra quelle ciglia vedo due fari
a meraviglia sereni e chiari.

I dream of marriage,
the candles lighting an airborne spirit
of love requited.
While they go crazy, we wander in bliss,
serene and lazy, gathering flowers of love.
Tell me again, is it true?
Yes, my dearest, I love only you,
Only you. Only, only you.

Ford:
La mia tattica maestra
le sue mosse pria registra.
Voi sarete l'ala destra,
noi sarem l'ala sinistra,
e costor con piè gagliardo
sfonderanno il baluardo.

Ford:
Neighbors, now that we have found him
bit by bit the plan enlarges.
From the right you circle round him;
from the left you lead the charges.
When supporting forces enter
we attack him from the center.

Tutti gli altri:
Bravo.

Others:
Count on us for satisfaction!

Dr. Cajus:
Bravo generale, aspettiamo un tuo segnale.

Dr. Caius:
You will sound the call to action.

Meg:
Il ribaldo vorrebbe un ventaglio.

Meg:
So we're expected to furnish a fan?

Falstaff:
Un breve spiraglio, non chiedo di più.

Falstaff:
I smother for air. I drown in these odors.

Quickly:
Ti metto il bavaglio se parli.

Quickly:
Speak another word and you're finished.

Ford:
Senti, accosta un po' l'orecchio!
Là c'è Alice e qua c'è il vecchio
seduttore. Essi credon d'esser soli
nel loro tenero abbandon.

Ford:
Put your ear a little closer.
They prepare their own undoing.
Now the turtle doves are cooing
but a storm will end the song.

Dr. Cajus:
Sento, intendo e vedo chiaro
delle femmine gl'inganni;
non vorrei, compare caro,
esser io ne' vostri panni.

Dr. Caius:
Listen, listen, I can hear them,
And all too clearly.
The skullduggery,
the deceit of all women!

Ford:
Zitto! A noi! Quest'è il momento.Zitto!
Attenti! Attenti a me.

Dr. Cajus:
Da' il segnal.

Ford:
Uno... Due... Tre...

Dr. Cajus:
Non è lui!

Tutti:
Sbalordimento!

Quickly, Meg, Alice, Falstaff:
Ouff! Cesto molesto!

Alice:
Silenzio!

Falstaff:
Protesto!

Meg e Quickly:
Che bestia restia!

Falstaff:
Portatemi via!

Meg:
È matto furibondo!

Falstaff:
Aiuto!

Alice, Meg e Quickly:
È il finimondo!

Nannetta e Fenton:
Dolci richiamid'amor.
Dimmi se m'ami!
Te bramo!

Ford:
Now is the moment.
Quiet! Attention!

Dr. Cajus:
Tell us when.

Ford:
One....two.....three....

Dr. Caius:
Who are they?

All:
Amazing!

Quickly, Meg, Alice, Falstaff:
Harassment!

Alice:
Quiet!

Falstaff:
I protest!

Meg and Quickly:
What a beast!

Falstaff:
I only want out!

Meg:
He's madder by the minute.

Falstaff:
Oh, spare me! Have mercy!

Alice, Meg and Quickly:
It's the end!

Nannetta and Fenton: *(the screen falls)*
Recall sweet love.
I love you, tell me you love me!
Yes, I love you!

Ford:

Ancor nuove rivolte!

Tu va' pe' fatti tuoi!
L'ho detto mille volte:
«Costei non fa per voi».

Bardolfo:
È là! Ferma!

Ford:
Dove?

Pistola:
Là!

Bardolfo:
Là! sulle scale.

Ford:
Squartatelo!

Tutti:
A caccia!

Quickly:
Che caccia infernale!

Alice:
Ned! Will! Tom! Isaac! Su! presto! presto!
Rovesciate quel cestodalla finestra
nell'acqua del fosso.
Là! Presso alle giuncaie,davanti al crocchio
delle lavandaie.

Nannetta:
C'è dentro un pezzo grosso.

Alice:
Tu chiama mio marito.
Gli narreremo il nostro caso pazzo.
Solo al vedere il cavalier nel guazzod'ogni
gelosa ubbia sarà guarito.

Quickly:
Pesa!

Ford:
(to Nannetta)
A waste of breath to scold you!
(to Fenton)
Be off, you're in the way!
I've told you a thousand times
my daughter's not for you.

Bardolph:
He's there! Stop him!

Ford:
Where?

Pistol:
There!

Bardolph:
Climbing the stairs.

Ford:
Go after him!

All:
Pursue him!

Quickly:
A mad hunting party!

Alice: *(to the servants)*
Ned! Will! Tom! Little Jack! Come! Hurry,
Take the basket and empty it into the river
near the bed of rushes,
the place where the women dump their
dirty linen.

Nannetta:
The basket is overloaded.

Alice: *(to Meg)*
Go call your master. When he sees the
dashing knight thrashing and splashing,
he'll reap some profit from Sir John's disaster.

Quickly: *(to the servants)*
Struggle!

Alice e Meg:
Coraggio!

Alice and Meg:
You'll manage! Keep trying!

Nannetta:
All fondo ha fatto crac!

Nannetta:
I heard the bottom pop.

Tutte:
Trionfo! Trionfo!Ah! Ah!

All:
A triumph! A triumph!

Alice:
Che tonfo!

Alice:
Triumph!

Nannetta e Meg:
Che tonfo!

Nannetta and Meg:
Triumph!

Tutte:
Patatrac!

All:
And ca-plop!

Th Windsor Wives had stuffed Falsatff into the laundry basket.
Servants raised the basktet up to the window and pushed it through —
right into the Thames river below.

END of ACT II

Act III — Scene 1
Falstaff has returned to the Garter Inn.
He concludes that the world is rundown place — a cesspool of iniquity,
a garden gone to seed, with no room for a virtuous man!
He is in a vile mood, foiled on the brink of success, scared out of his wits, stuffed into a
laundry basket of foul linen, nearly suffocated, then dumped into the river.

Outside the Garter Inn, Falstaff is seated alone, and in a somber mood.
He rouses himself, and summons the host.

Falstaff:
Ehi taverniere!

Falstaff:
Hey! Get a move on!

Mondo ladro. Mondo rubaldo.
Reo mondo!
Taverniere: un bicchier di vin caldo.

World of riff raff! World of corruption!
All rotten!
Bring me a pitcher. Make it hot and mellow.

Io, dunque, avrò vissuto tanti anni, audace e
destro cavaliere, per essere portato in un
canestro
e gittato al canale co' pannilini biechi,
come si fa coi gatti e i catellini ciechi.

Outrageous! After long years of service,
a cavalier, a fearless fighter, is folded up
and stuffed into a basket with a foul load of
linen and tossed into the river,
discarded like a litter of defective puppies.

Ché se non galleggiava per me quest'epa
tronfia, certo affogavo. Brutta morte.
L'acqua mi gonfia.

Had not my belly saved me,
ballooning like a buoy, I'd have gone under,
soaked in water, swollen and bloated.

Mondo reo. Non c'è più virtù.
Tutto declina.
Va', vecchio John, va', va' per la tua via;
cammina finché tu muoia.
Allor scomparirà la vera virilità del mondo.
Che giorna taccia nera!
M'aiuti il ciel! Impinguo troppo.
Ho dei peli grigi.

World of scum! Garden gone to seed.
Where now is virtue?
Go, old Sir John, go, go, old and unwanted,
to death just around the corner.
The last remains of manhood vanishes.
I was so close to winning!
But it was the worst day yet!
I just get fatter while my hair keeps thinning.

Versiamo un po' di vino nell'acqua del
Tamigi!
Buono. Ber del vino dolce e sbottonarsi al
sole, dolce cosa!
Il buon vino sperde le tetre fole dello
sconforto, accende l'occhio e il pensier, dal
labbro sale al cervel e quivi risveglia il
picciol fabbro dei trilli; un negro grillo che
vibra entro l'uom brillo.
Trilla ogni fibra in cor, l'allegro etere al trillo
guizza e il giocondo globo squilibra una
demenza trillante! E il trillo invade il mondo!

To the waters of the Thames let us add a
touch of sherry again.
Splendid, for wine is warmer than the glow
of sunshine.
See how it lights up the eye,
revives and kindles the brain,
the inner chirping of sweet intoxication.
Filling the soul with song,
a light-hearted breeze, mellow and balmy,
makes the entire globe sing along,
led by a wine-swilling goblin
that heads a willing army!

Alice, Nannetta, Meg, Mr. Ford, Dr. Caius and Fenton spy on Falstaff,
and overhear Dame Quickly as she addresses Falstaff.

Quickly:
Reverenza. La bella Alice

Falstaff:
Al diavolo te con Alice bella!
Ne ho piene le bisacce! Ne ho piene le
budella!

Quickly:
Voi siete errato.

Falstaff:
Un canchero!
Sento ancor le cornate
di quell'irco geloso!
Ho ancor l'ossa arrembate
d'esser rimasto curvo,
come una buona lama di Bilbao,
nello spazio d'un panierin di dama!
Con quel tufo! E quel caldo!
Un uom della mia tempra,
che in uno stillicidio continuo si distempra!
Poi, quando fui ben cotto,
rovente, incandescente,
m'han tuffato nell'acqua. Canaglie!

Quickly: *(entering, bowing)*
Reverence! Our lovely Alice.

Falstaff:
To blazes with you and your lovely Alice!
I'm on to your conniving,
your treachery and malice.

Quickly:
A dreadful error.

Falstaff:
That Jezebel!
I'm in shock, badly shaken,
buried live in a basket.
Oh. the toll that love has taken.
Crouching beneath the bedding!
A fattened heifer heading
for the butcher's block.
This torture was the limit.
By nature I'm a man
sweating buckets by the minute.
Then to make the story shorter,
when roasted and suffocated.
Worst of all, freezing water! Vultures!

Alice, Meg, Nannetta, Fenton, Dr. Caius and Ford, one by one,
peer out from hiding. They listen briefly, then hide again.

Quickly:
Essa è innocente.
Prendete abbaglio.

Falstaff:
Vattene!

Quickly:
La colpa è di quei fanti
malaugurati! Alice piange, urla, invoca i
santi.
Povera donna! V"ama. Leggete.

Alice:
Legge.

Quickly:
But she is blameless, entirely blameless!
You're much mistaken.

Falstaff:
Off with you!

Quickly:
Those idiotic servants made such a blunder.
Poor, wretched Alice! Weeping,
her eyes toward heaven, her heart torn
asunder. Read this! She loves you!

Alice: *(watching him read the letter)*
Read it!

Ford:
Legge.

Nannetta:
Vedrai che ci ricasca.

Alice:
L'uom non si corregge.

Meg:
Nasconditi.

Dr. Cajus:
Rilegge.

Ford:
Rilegge. L'esca inghiotte.

Falstaff:
«T'aspetterò nel parco real, a mezzanotte.
Tu verrai travestito da cacciatore nero
alla quercia di Herne»

Quickly:
Amor ama il mistero.
Per rivedervi, Alice si val d'una leggenda
popolar. Quella quercia è un luogo da
tregenda.
Il cacciatore nero s'è impeso ad un suo
ramo.
V'ha chi crede vederlo ricomparir

Falstaff:
Entriamo.
Là si discorre meglio. Narrami la tua frasca.

Quickly:
Quando il rintocco della mezzanotte...

Alice:
Quando il rintocco della mezzanotte
cupo si sparge nel silente orror,
sorgon gli spirti vagabondi a frotte
e vien nel parco il nero cacciator.
Egli cammina lento, lento, lento,
nel gran letargo della sepoltura.
S'avanza livido...

Ford:
Read!

Nannetta:
It's looking better to him.

Alice:
He has not learned his lesson.

Meg:
Stay out of sight.

Dr. Caius:
Reread it!

Ford:
The letter. Let us listen.

Falstaff: *(reading)*
"I'll be waiting for you in the Royal Park
underneath the spreading oak of the Herne.
Come disguised as the Black Knight."

Quickly:
Romance revels in mystery.
Eager to please, a bit overbold,
Alice recalled a tale of old,
for the oak's a place bewitched and haunted.
The Black Knight's body dangled,
found hanging from its branches.
His ghost wanders there nightly.

Falstaff:
Inside, we can pursue the matter.
More of this bedtime story.

Quickly:
When midnight chimes the witching hour...

Alice:
When midnight chimes the witching hour...
joined by the Black Knight
returning from the dead.
as he advances slowly, slowly, slowly,
like death itself,
whose horrors none should utter,
as he approaches stealthily...

Nannetta:
Oh! Che spavento!

Meg:
Già sento il brivido della paura!

Alice:
Fandonie che ai bamboli
raccontan le nonne
con lunghi preamboli,
per farli dormir.

Alice, Nannetta, Meg:
Vendetta di donne
non deve fallir.

Alice:
S'avanza livido e il passo converge
al tronco ove esalò l'anima prava.
Sbucan le fate. Sulla fronte egli erge
due corna lunghe, lunghe, lunghe.

Ford:
Brava.
Quelle corna saranno la mia gioia!

Alice:
Bada! tu pur ti meriti
qualche castigatoia!

Ford:
Perdona. Riconosco i miei demeriti.

Alice:
Ma guai se ancor ti coglie
quella mania feroce
di cercar dentro il guscio d'una noce
l'amante di tua moglie.
Ma il tempo stringe e vuol fantasia lesta.

Meg:
Affrettiam.

Fenton:
Concertiam la mascherata.

Alice:
Nannetta!

Nannetta:
By all that's holy!

Meg:
Frozen with fear, I shiver and I shudder.

Alice:
Palaver for little ones
concocted by nurses,
cadavers and curses
to send them to sleep.

Alice, Nannetta, Meg:
We women will keep
this moonlight meeting.

Alice:
He approaches the horrid place stealthily.
Now pale with anger, he clutches his brow,
for on his ghostly forehead
two horns grow longer, longer, longer.

Ford:
Brava!
Horns that some other men must wear!

Alice: *(to Ford)*
Careful! Do not scorn a punishment
you well deserve to share.

Ford:
Oh, pardon! My fault, I now am penitent.

Alice:
Beware! You'll suffer much
if you attempt this intrigue again:
seeking your wife's latest lover.
But we must hurry,
for time is ever fleeting.

Meg:
Let's hurry!

Fenton:
Let's prepare for this midnight meeting.

Alice: *(to Nannetta)*
My darling.

Nannetta:
Eccola qua!

Alice:
Sarai la fata
regina delle fate, in bianca veste
chiusa in candido vel, cinta di rose.

Nannetta:
E canterò parole armoniose.

Alice:
Tu la verde sarai ninfa silvana,
e la comare Quickly una befana.
Scende la sera, la scena si oscura.

Nannetta:
A meraviglia!

Alice:
Avrò con me dei putti che fingeran folletti,
e spiritelli, e diavoletti, e pipistrelli,
e farfarelli.
Su Falstaff camuffato in manto e corni
ci scaglieremo tutti e lo tempesteremo
finch'abbia confessata la sua perversità.
Poi ci smaschereremo e, pria che il ciel
raggiorni, la giuliva brigata se ne ritornerà.

Meg:
Vien sera. Rincasiam.

Alice:
L'appuntamento è alla quercia di Herne.

Fenton:
È inteso.

Nannetta:
A meraviglia!
Oh che allegro spavento!

Alice, Nannetta, Nannetta, Fenton:
Addio.

Alice:
Provvedi le lanterne.

Nannetta:
Ready for sport.

Alice: *(to Nannetta)*
You shall be Queen of the fairies,
in a veil as white as mother of pearl
sprinkled with roses.

Nannetta:
My realm of song when all nature reposes.

Alice: *(to Meg)*
You are the green Nymph of the forest.
What role for good friend Quickly?
The Witch of Windsor!

Nannetta:
Gala performance!

Alice:
A pick of playful pixies
will populate our revels,
with a pack of imps and devils
all intent on mischief making.
With Falstaff on the scene in horns and
mantle, we'll surround him.
Then we will discard him, well spent,
before the night sky is over.

Meg:
But meanwhile lots to do!

Alice:
We'll gather beneath the oak tree.

Fenton:
By moonlight.

Nannetta:
Marvelous! A combination of fun, romance
and adventure.

Alice, Nannetta, Nannetta, Fenton:
Till later.

Alice: *(calling after Meg)*
More lanterns will be needed.

As they leave, Quickly exits the inn.
She sees Ford and Dr. Caius talking together, and pauses to eavesdrop.

Ford:
Non dubitar, tu sposerai mia figlia.
Rammenti bene il suo travestimento?

Dr. Cajus:
Cinta di rose, il vel bianco e la vesta.

Alice:
Non ti scordar le maschere.

Meg:
No, certo.
Né tu le raganelle!

Ford:
Io già disposi
la rete mia. Sul finir della festa
verrete a me col volto ricoperto
essa dal vel, tu da un mantel fantesco
e vi benedirò come due sposi.

Dr. Cajus:
Siam d'accordo.

Quickly:
(Stai fresco!)
Nannetta! Ohè! Nannetta!

Nannetta:
Che c'è? Che c'è?

Quickly:
Prepara la canzone della fata.

Nannetta:
È preparata.

Alice:
Tu, non tardar.

Quickly:
Chi prima arriva, aspetta.

Ford:
Sir, have no fear. You'll wed my daughter
tonight, though in disguise.

Dr. Caius:
Girded with roses, white veil and gown.

Alice: *(within)*
Bring along capes and camouflage.

Meg:
With rattles. And you bring sticks and
whistles.

Ford:
The ball is rolling, my plan is on target.
When it's over bring Anne to me,
your faces both well covered,
hers with a veil, yours with a friar's mantle.
I'll then sanction the marriage.

Dr. Caius:
Neat and simple.

Quickly: *(overhearing the two men)*
(You think so!)
Where are you? Anne! Oh, Anne! Pst!

Nannetta: *(within)*
Who calls? Who calls?

Quickly:
Prepare your song as the Fairy Queen.

Nannetta: *(within)*
I've done so already.

Alice: *(also within)*
Let's not be late.

Quickly:
We'll see which man she marries!

Act III — Scene 2

*It is nearly midnight. There is a pale moonlight, barely visible
in the Royal Park of Windsor near the giant oak tree of Huntsman Herne,
the ghostly habitat of goblins, witches, elves and demons.*

In the distance, the far off cries of watchmen are heard. Fenton enters.

Fenton: **Fenton:**

Dal labbro il canto estasiato vola
pe' silenzi notturni e va lontano
e alfin ritrova un altro labbro umano
che gli risponde co' la sua parola.

Allor la nota che non è più sola
vibra di gioia in un accordo arcano
e innamorando l'aer antelucano
con altra voce al suo fonte rivola.

Quivi ripiglia suon, ma la sua cura
tende sempre ad unir chi lo disuna.
Così baciai la disiata bocca!
Bocca baciata non perde ventura.

Nannetta:
Anzi rinnova come fa la luna.

Fenton:
Ma il canto muor nel bacio che lo tocca.

My song of rapture rises into the dark,
floating over the silent forest shadows
to where I hear another blending voice,
two voices sweetly responding.

It's no longer a lonely signal in the night;
instead, a soothing harmony has sounded.
The drowsy dawn air comes alive,
reawakened by the echoes of love.

We sing, breathing as one, ending exalted
in the flame of a kiss, given and taken,
as our lips touch one another
they remain enchanted forever.

Nannetta: *(within)*
Ever reborn like the splendor of the moon.

Fenton:
The throbbing song ends as lips come closer.

*Nannetta embraces Fenton. Alice enters with Quickly.
Fenton puts on the black robe of a friar.*

Alice:
No signore! Tu indossa questa cappa.

Fenton:
Che vuol dir ciò?

Nannetta:
Lasciati fare.

Alice:
Ask no questions, just slip into this robe.

Fenton:
What does this mean?

Nannetta:
You will know later.

Alice:
Allaccia.

Alice: *(handing Fenton a mask)*
This too.

Nannetta:
È un fraticel sgusciato dalla trappa.

Nannetta: *(looking him over)*
A roving monk who left the sheltered cloister.

Alice:
Il tradimento che Ford ne minaccia
tornar deve in suo scorno e in nostro aiuto.

Alice:
We shall turn my husband's sly maneuvers
to our own sweet advantage.

Fenton:
Spiegatevi.

Fenton:
Explain yourself.

Alice:
Ubbidisci presto e muto.
L'occasïone come viene scappa.
Chi vestirai da finta sposa?

Alice: *(to Quickly)*
Trust us, tomorrow may be too late.
it's now or never to play your role:
Who is going to be our fake bride?

Quickly:
Un gaio ladron nasuto che aborre il Dottor
Cajo.

Quickly:
A rogue with a big red nose
who abhors the crusty doctor!

Meg:
Ho nascosto i folletti lungo il fosso.
Siam pronte.

Meg: *(rushing to Alice)*
I've hidden imps and goblins in the hedges.
We're ready.

Alice:
Zitto. Viene il pezzo grosso.
Via!

Alice: *(listening)*
Quiet! Here comes the horned hunter.
Hurry!

Falstaff enters. He is wrapped in a voluminous mantle, with two stag horns on his head.
The chimes of midnight begin to sound.

Falstaff:
Una, due, tre, quattro, cinque, sei, sette
botte, otto, nove, dieci, undici, dodici.
Mezzanotte.
Questa è la quercia.
Numi, proteggetemi!
Giove! Tu per amor d'Europa ti
trasformasti in bove,
portasti corna. I numi c'insegnan la
modestia.
L'amore metamorfosa un uom in una bestia.
Odo un soave passo!

Alice! Amor ti chiama!
Vieni! l'amor m'infiamma!

Falstaff:
One, two, three, four, five, six, stroke of
seven, ten, eleven, twelve o'clock.
Midnight!
And here's the oak tree.
Mighty gods, oh smile on me.
To attain Europa, Jove himself became a
horned bull,
and overpowered, inspired.
Am I to be a coward?
Love has made an amazing transformation.
I hear steps approaching...
(Alice appears)
Dear Alice! By love transported.
Closer! I burn with passion.

Alice:
Sir John!

Falstaff:
Sei la mia dama!

Alice:
Sir John!

Falstaff:
Sei la mia damma!

Alice:
O sfavillante amor!

Falstaff:
Vieni! Già fremo e fervo!

Alice:
Sir John!

Falstaff:
Sono il tuo servo!
Sono il tuo cervo,
imbizzarrito.
Ed or piovan tartufi,
rafani e finocchi!
E sian la mia pastura!
E amor trabocchi!
Siam soli!

Alice:
No. Qua nella selva densa
mi segue Meg.

Falstaff:
È doppia l'avventura!
Venga anche lei! Squartatemi
come un camoscio a mensa!
Sbranatemi! Cupido
alfin mi ricompensa.
Io t'amo! t'amo!

Meg:
Aiuto!

Alice:
Un grido! Ahimè!

Alice:
Sir John!

Falstaff:
My inspiration!

Alice:
Sir John!

Falstaff:
My summer flower!

Alice:
You are my noble deer!

Falstaff:
Closer! Come to my embraces.

Alice: *(always avoiding his embrace)*
Sir John!

Falstaff:
I am a beast,
held in your power,
conquered by beauty.
Let the sky rain potatoes,
cabbages and turnips,
on higher food I flourish.
On love I feast!
Are we alone here?

Alice:
No! There, in the woods
I've spotted my neighbor Meg.

Falstaff:
Divide me down the middle;
my size and scope are double.
There's room for both.
The best for you, the rest for her.
Sly Cupid rewards my trouble.
So onward! So onward! I love you!

Meg: *(within)*
The goblins!

Alice: *(pretending terror)*
A cry of alarm!

Meg:
Vien la tregenda!

Alice:
Ahimè! Fuggiamo!

Falstaff:
Dove?

Alice:
Il cielo perdoni al mio peccato!

Falstaff:
Il diavol non vuol ch'io sia dannato.

Nannetta:
Ninfe! Elfi! Silfi! Doridi! Sirene!
L'astro degli incantesimi in cielo è sorto.

Nannetta:
Sorgete! Ombre serene!

Falstaff:
Sono le fate. Chi le guarda è morto.

Meg: *(within)*
Run for your lives!

Alice:
Oh Lord! Forgive me!

Falstaff:
Goblins!

Alice: *(as she flees)*
May heaven pardon my transgression!

Falstaff:
I would have gladly yielded to temptation!

Nannetta: *(from inside)*
Goblins! Gremlins! Pixies! Sorcerers! Sirens!
The rays of our enchanted star shine down.

Nannetta: *(from within)*
Arise! Serene shadows!

Falstaff: *(throwing himself to the ground)*
Demons and fairies! To look once, you die.

Nannetta appears as the Queen of the Fairies; Meg as the Green Nymph; Alice as a fairy;
Bardolph in monk's habit, cowl pulled down, but unmasked; Dr. Caius in grey habit,
also unmasked; Fenton in black habit but with a mask; Pistol as a satyr;
little girls dressed as fairies, white and blue, nymphs, elves and imps.

Falstaff remains motionless, face down.

Alice:
Inoltriam.

Nannetta:
Egli è là.

Alice:
Steso al suol.

Nannetta:
Lo confonde il terror.

Fate:
Si nasconde!

Alice: *(coming forward)*
Follow me.

Nannetta: *(upon seeing Falstaff)*
There he lies!

Alice:
Facing down.

Nannetta:
Frightened out of his mind.

Spirits:
He is hiding.

Alice:
Non ridiam!

Alice: *(before leaving)*
Mustn't clown.

Fate:
Non ridiam!

Spirits:
No, no, no!

Nannetta:
Tutte qui, dietro a me. Cominciam.

Nannetta:
Form a circle, and then we begin!

Fate:
Tocca a te.

Spirits:
You say when.

Nannetta:

Nannetta: *(the Queen of the Fates)*

Sul fil d'un soffio etesio
scorrete, agili larve,
fra i rami un baglior cesio
d'alba lunare apparve.
Danzate! e il passo blando
misuri un blando suon,
le magiche accoppiando
carole alla canzon.

The boughs and bushes tremble,
in breezes light as gossamer.
Hurry, before the moon is down,
elves of the night, assemble!
You dancers, follow the music
that guides our fairy throng.
Magic and grace are blended
when dance adorns the song.

Fate:
La selva dorme e sperde
incenso ed ombra; e par
nell'aer denso un verde
asilo in fondo al mar.

Fairies:
The forest slumbers,
subdued in the shadow of shrouded trees.
The heavy air envelops
a sylvan scene beneath the seas.

Nannetta:
Erriam sotto la luna
scegliendo fior da fiore,
ogni corolla in core
porta la sua fortuna.
Coi gigli e le vïole
scriviam dei nomi arcani,
dalle fatate mani
germoglino parole.
Parole alluminate
di puro argento e d'or,
carmi e malie. Le fate
hanno per cifre i fior.

Nannetta:
We wander by moonlight
and roam among the flowers,
gathering nectar with healing powers
from each blossom.
We gather our fairy spells
of daisies and of primroses,
our sacred book reposes,
held in a sprig of heather.
For you that dare to enter,
eager to come and see
our domain of wonder,
flowers contain the key.

Fate:
Moviamo ad una ad una
sotto il lunare albor,
verso la quercia bruna
del nero cacciator.

Spirits:
Before the moon goes under
we cross through moss and fern
toward the oak of the hunter
bearing the name of Herne.

Bardolfo:
Alto là!

Bardolph:
Spirits, halt!

Pistola:
Chi va là?

Pistol:
Who is that?

Falstaff:
Pietà!

Falstaff:
Mercy!

Quickly:
C'è un uom!

Quickly:
A human!

Alice, Meg, Nannetta:
C'è un uom!

Alice, Meg, Nannetta:
A man! A man!

Ford:
Cornuto come un bue!

Ford:
The horns denote the devil.

Pistola:
Rotondo come un pomo!

Pistol:
A mortal or a mountain?

Bardolfo:
Grosso come una nave!

Bardolph:
Get him ready for roasting.

Pistola e Bardolfo:
Alzati, olà!

Pistol and Bardolph:
Man or beast! Stand up!

Falstaff:
Portatemi una grue!
Non posso.

Falstaff:
You'll need a crane for hoisting
the body.

Ford:
È troppo grave.

Ford:
Too heavy to handle.

Quickly:
È corrotto!

Quickly:
He is tainted.

Fate:
È corrotto!

Others:
And polluted.

Bardolfo:
È impuro!

Bardolph:
He needs a thorough cleaning.

Alice:
Evita il tuo periglio.
Già il Dottor Cajo ti cerca.

Nannetta:
Troviamo un nascondiglio.

Quickly:
Poi tornerete lesti al mio richiamo.

Bardolfo:
Spiritelli! Folletti!
Farfarelli! Vampiri! Agili insetti
del palude infernale! Punzecchiatelo!
Orticheggiatelo! Martirizzatelo
coi grifi aguzzi!
Accorrono velocissimi alcuni
ragazzi vestiti da folletti,
e si scagliano su Falstaff.

Falstaff:
Ahimè! tu puzzi
come una puzzola.

Folletti e Diavoli:
Ruzzola, ruzzola, ruzzola, ruzzola!

Alice, Quickly, Meg:
Pizzica, pizzica,
pizzica, stuzzica,
spizzica, spizzica,
pungi, spilluzzica,
finch'egli abbai!

Falstaff:
Ahi! Ahi! Ahi! Ahi!

Folletti e Diavoli:
Scrolliam crepitacoli,
scarandole e nacchere!
Di schizzi e di zacchere
quell'otre si macoli.
Meniam scorribandole, danziamo la tresca,
treschiam le farandole sull'ampia ventresca.
Zanzare ed assilli, volate alla lizza
coi dardi e gli spilli!
Ch'ei crepi di stizza!

Alice: *(aside, to Nannetta)*
Daughter, a word of warning,
for Dr. Caius comes hunting.

Nannetta: *(with Fenton)*
We'd better go into hiding.

Quickly:
But stay alert, and come back when I call.

Bardolph: *(exorcising over Falstaff's body)*
Elfin creatures! Mosquitoes!
Angry hornets and vampires!
Come, bugs and bats
recruited from bog and belfry.
Pinch and pummel him,
pepper and pickle him,
prick out his vanity,
needle and nettle.

Falstaff: *(to Bardolph)*
Ah, me! Your smell will first drive me to
insanity.

Imps and Elves:
Rumple and tumble him!

Alice, Quickly, Meg:
Prick at him,
tickle him,
needle and nettle him.
Hassle and heckle
till you unsettle him.

Falstaff:
Ahi! Ahi! Ahi! Ahi!

Imps and Elves:
We elfins will rumple
and tumble him.
A rare chance
to hassle and humble him.
Adopt a stronger line,
and turn him to jelly
by forming a line across his big belly.
You swamp flies and mosquitoes,
this mass of libidos is yet to cry uncle.

Alice, Meg, Quickly:
Pizzica, pizzica,
pizzica, stuzzica,
spizzica, spizzica,
pungi, spilluzzica
finch'egli abbai!

Dr. Cajus e Ford:
Cialtron!

Bardolfo e Pistola:
Poltron! Ghiotton!

Ford:
Pancia ritronfia!

Alice:
Guancia rigonfia!

Bardolfo:
Sconquassaletti!

Quickly:
Spaccafarsetti!

Pistola:
Vuotabarili!

Dr. Cajus:
Sfiancagiumenti!

Ford:
Triplice mento!

Bardolfo e Pistola:
Di' che ti penti!

Falstaff:
Ahi! Ahi! mi pento!
Tu puti d'acquavita.
Ma salvagli l'addomine.

Dr. Cajus, Ford, Bardolfo, Pistola:
Monte d'obesità, rispondi.

Falstaff:
Ben mi sta.

Alice, Meg, Quickly:
Smack, whack him,
keep on attacking him;
turn diabolical.
Frazzle and frighten him
and thus enlighten him.

Dr. Caius and Ford:
You swill!

Bardolph and Pistol:
You swine!

Ford:
Cowardly custard.

Alice:
Blusterer.

Bardolph:
Lord of the gluttons.

Quickly:
Burster of buttons.

Pistol:
Would-be seducer.

Dr. Caius:
Big for your breeches.

Ford:
Grasper at riches.

Bardolph:
Reform or you'll be sorry.

Falstaff:
Yes, I'll reform, but not today.
Oh, praise the Lord, but pass the wine.
I'll sin, but only now and then.

Dr. Caius, Ford, Bardolph, Pistol:
Answer, mountain of obesity.

Falstaff:
How well you put it.

Bardolfo:
Re dei cornuti!

Falstaff:
Va' via, tu puti.

Tutti:
Furfanteria!

Falstaff:
Ahi! Così sia.

Bardolfo:
Ed or che il diavol ti porti via!

Falstaff:
Nitro! Catrame e solfo!
Riconosco Bardolfo!
Naso vermiglio!
Nasobargiglio!
Puntuta lesina!
Vampa di resina!
Salamandra! Ignis fatuus! Vecchia alabarda!
Stecca di sartore! Schidion d'inferno!
Aringa secca!
Vampiro! Basilisco!
Manigoldo! Ladrone!
Ho detto. E se mentisco
voglio che mi si spacchi il cinturone!

Tutti:
Bravo!

Falstaff:
Un poco di pausa. Sono stanco.

Quickly:
Vieni, Ti coprirò col velo bianco.

Bardolph:
King of the rounded!

Falstaff:
Your breath, no doubt, will knock me out.

All:
So dissipated! Degenerated! Over-inflated!

Falstaff:
What if I am?

Bardolph: *(his mask falls off)*
You and your luggage can go to the devil.

Falstaff:
Viper! Imposter! Traitor!
You're the purse snatcher Bardolph!
Two-legged adder! Rat from the gutter!
Blot on humanity! Walking obscenity!
Scrawny beggar! Puny parasite!
You caterpillar.
Sack and sherry swiller,
You fever blister, you wheezy fiddle.
You scaly, creepy, crawly, slimy lizard!
You vermin!
You heard me, and if unjust,
divide me in two
and slice me down the middle.

All: *(except Bardolph)*
Bravo!

Falstaff:
I need time for breathing. What a night!

Quickly: *(softly, to Bardolph)*
Come, it is time to don that veil of white.

Dr. Caius; Quickly and Bardolph disappear behind the trees.

Ford:
Ed or, mentre vi passa la scalmana,
sir John, dite: il cornuto chi è?

Alice e Meg:
Chi è?

Ford: *(to Falstaff with an ironical bow)*
Well, well! After some time to think it over,
Sir John, tell me, who now wears the horns?

Alice and Meg:
Who now? Who now? Who now?

Alice:
Vi siete fatto muto?

Falstaff:
Caro signor Fontana!

Alice:
Sbagliate nel saluto.
Questi è Ford, mio marito.

Quickly:
Cavaliero,
voi credeste due donne così grulle,
così citrulle,
da darsi anima e corpo all'avversiero,
per un uom vecchio, sudicio ed obeso.

Meg e Quickly:
Con quella testa calva.

Alice:
E con quel peso!

Falstaff:
Incomincio ad accorgermi
d'esser stato un somaro.

Alice:
E un cervo.

Ford:
Un bue.

Falstaff:
Ogni sorta di gente dozzinale
mi beffa e se ne gloria;
pur, senza me, costor con tanta boria
non avrebbero un briciol di sale.
Son io che vi fa scaltri.
L'arguzia mia crea l'arguzia degli altri.

Tutti:
Ma bravo!

Ford:
Per gli dèi!
Se non ridessi ti sconquasserei!

Alice:
You seem a little shaken.

Falstaff:
Ah, Mister Brooke, here also...

Alice:
The name you have mistaken.
Mister Ford. my dear husband.

Quickly: *(reappearing)*
Sir, with deference.
So you fancied two women so dimwitted
that they were ready to fall head over heels,
hook, line and sinker for an old clinker
gone to seed and sweat.

Meg and Quickly:
With that bald head.

Alice:
A donkey!

Falstaff:
But I'm starting to see
that I'm less of a lion than an ass.

Alice:
It's a deer.

Ford:
An ox.

Falstaff:
All this rabble belittle, mock and malign me.
Fools that they are!
For I'm not only witty in myself,
but I create the wit in others.
Yes, I supply the seasoning,
the zest and flavor for you lesser mortals.

Others:
Well-spoken!

Ford:
That will do.
Shut up before I salt and pepper you!

Ma basta. Ed ora vo' che m'ascoltiate.	But onward: gather round for celebration.
Coronerem la mascherata bella	Our masquerade draws near a grand
co' gli sponsali della	conclusion:
regina delle fate.	Hail the betrothal of our Queen of the Fairies!

Enter Dr. Caius, disguised, hand in hand with Bardolph, veiled in white as Queen of the Fairies.

Ford:

Già s'avanza la coppia degli sposi.
Attenti!

Ford:

Let us welcome the couple getting married.
Attention!

Tutti:

Attenti!

All:

A wedding!

Ford:

Eccola, in bianca vesta
col velo e il serto delle rose in testa
e il fidanzato suo ch'io le disposi.
Circondatela, o ninfe.

Ford:

Look at her! A radiant virgin in veil of white
and garlanded with roses.
A lucky man claims her
for his own in marriage!

*Alice presents Nannetta and Fenton, Nannetta wearing a
thick blue veil, Fenton a dark habit and mask.*

Alice:

Un'altra coppia d'amanti desïosi
chiede d'essere ammessa agli augurosi
connubi!

Alice:

Another couple of lovers come here
pleading, eager to be admitted into the holy
bonds of marriage.

Ford:

E sia. Farem la festa doppia.
Avvicinate i lumi.
Il ciel v'accoppia.

Ford:

Delighted! Tonight a double wedding!
So bring the lanterns closer.
Empowered by heaven

Giù le maschere e i veli. Apoteosi!

Off with disguises!

*At a sign from Ford, masks and veils are all removed, to great laughter,
except from Dr. Caius, Bardolph and Ford.*

Dr. Cajus:

Spavento!

Dr. Caius:

Oh, horror!

Ford:

Tradimento!

Ford:

Revolution!

Tutti:

Apoteosi!

Others:

Apotheosis!

Ford:

Fenton con mia figlia!

Ford:

Fenton and my daughter!

Dr. Cajus:
Ho sposato Bardolfo!

Dr. Caius:
I am married to Bardolph!

Tutti:
Ah! Ah!

Others:
Evviva! Evviva!

Dr. Cajus:
Spavento!

Dr. Caius:
How frightening!

Le Donne:
Vittoria!

Women:
Triumph!

Tutti:
Evviva! Evviva!

All:
Hail!

Ford:
Oh! Meraviglia!

Ford: *(stupefied)*
Have I gone crazy?

Alice:
L'uom cade spesso nelle reti ordite
dalle malizie sue.

Alice:
Be wary when you weave a trap for others
lest you entrap the weaver.

Falstaff:
Caro buon messer Ford, ed ora, dite:
lo scornato chi è?

Falstaff:
Ah, dear old Mister Ford! I pose the
question: Who now plays the fool?

Ford:
Lui.

Ford: *(pointing to Caius)*
Him.

Dr. Cajus:
Tu.

Dr. Caius: *(pointing to Ford)*
You.

Ford:
No.

Ford:
No.

Dr. Cajus:
Sì.

Dr. Caius:
Me?

Bardolfo:
Voi.

Bardolph:
Both.

Falstaff:
Tutti e due.

Falstaff:
There's your answer.

Alice:
No. Tutti e tre.

Volgiti e mira quelle ansie leggiadre.

Alice: *(including Falstaff)*
No! Three at least!
(to Ford)
So in love, so devoted!

Nannetta:
Perdonateci, padre.

Ford:
Chi schivare non può la propria noia
l'accetti di buon grado.
Facciamo il parentado
e che il ciel vi dia gioia.

Tutti:
Evviva!

Falstaff:
Un coro e terminiam la scena.

Ford:
E poi con sir Falstaff, tutti, andiamo a cena.

Falstaff:

Nannetta:
Pardon, pardon, oh father!

Ford:
Out maneuvered, out smarted and out
voted, I'd better cry surrender.
Receive a father's blessing
and the blessing of heaven.

All:
Hail!

Falstaff:
A choral fugue will end the caper.

Ford:
Lead on, Sir Falstaff, then off to supper.

Falstaff:

Tutto nel mondo è burla.
L'uom è nato burlone,
la fede in cor gli ciurla,
gli ciurla la ragione.
Tutti gabbati! Irride
l'un l'altro ogni mortal.
Ma ride ben chi ride
la risata final.

Life is a laughing matter,
man a bundle of folly,
full of clamor and clatter, idle chatter,
whether gloomy or jolly, lowly or mighty,
fickle and flighty,
we jesters are prone to bicker and brawl.
Ah, but the question yet festers:
Who will laugh last of all?

END of OPERA

DICTIONARY OF OPERA AND MUSICAL TERMS

Accelerando - Play the music faster, but gradually.

Adagio - At a slow or gliding tempo, not as slow as largo, but not as fast as andante.

Agitato - Restless or agitated.

Allegro - At a brisk or lively tempo, faster than andante but not as fast as presto.

Andante - A moderately slow, easy-going tempo.

Appoggiatura - An extra or embellishing note preceding a main melodic note. Usually written as a note of smaller size, it shares the time value of the main note.

Arabesque - Flourishes or fancy patterns usually applying to vocal virtuosity.

Aria - A solo song usually structured in a formal pattern. Arias generally convey reflective and introspective thoughts rather than descriptive action.

Arietta - A shortened form of aria.

Arioso - A musical passage or composition having a mixture of free recitative and metrical song.

Arpeggio - Producing the tones of a chord in succession rather than simultaneously.

Atonal - Music that is not anchored in traditional musical tonality; it does not use the diatonic scale and has no keynote or tonal center.

Ballad opera - Eighteenth-century English opera consisting of spoken dialogue and music derived from popular ballad and folksong sources. The most famous is *The Beggar's Opera,* which is a satire of the Italian opera seria.

Bar - A vertical line across the stave that divides the music into measures.

Baritone - A male singing voice ranging between bass and tenor.

Baroque - A style of artistic expression prevalent in the 17th century that is marked by the use of complex forms, bold ornamentation, and florid decoration. The Baroque period extends from approximately 1600 to 1750 and includes the works of the original creators of modern opera, the Camerata, as well as the later works by Bach and Handel.

Bass - The lowest male voice, usually divided into categories such as:

> **Basso buffo** - A bass voice that specializes in comic roles: Dr. Bartolo in Rossini's *The Barber of Seville.*

> **Basso cantante** - A bass voice that demonstrates melodic singing quality: King Philip in Verdi's *Don Carlos.*

> **Basso profundo** - the deepest, most profound, or most dramatic of bass voices: Sarastro in Mozart's *The Magic Flute.*

Bel canto - Literally, "beautiful singing." It originated in Italian opera of the 17th and 18th centuries and stressed beautiful tones produced with ease, clarity, purity, and evenness, together with an agile vocal technique and virtuosity. Bel canto flourished in the first half of the 19th century in the works of Rossini, Bellini, and Donizetti.

Cabaletta - A lively, concluding portion of an aria or duet. The term is derived from the Italian word "cavallo," or horse: it metaphorically describes a horse galloping to the finish line.

Cadenza - A flourish or brilliant part of an aria (or concerto) commonly inserted just before a finale. It is usually performed without accompaniment.

Camerata - A gathering of Florentine writers and musicians between 1590 and 1600 who attempted to recreate what they believed was the ancient Greek theatrical synthesis of drama, music, and stage spectacle; their experimentation led to the creation of the early structural forms of modern opera.

Cantabile - An indication that the singer should sing sweetly.

Cantata - A choral piece generally containing Scriptural narrative texts: the *St. Matthew Passion* of Bach.

Cantilena - Literally, "little song." A lyrical melody meant to be played or sung "cantabile," or with sweetness and expression.

Canzone - A short, lyrical operatic song usually containing no narrative association with the drama but rather simply reflecting the character's state of mind: Cherubino's "Voi che sapete" in Mozart's *The Marriage of Figaro.*

Castrato - A young male singer who was surgically castrated to retain his treble voice.

Cavatina - A short aria popular in 18th and 19th century opera that usually heralded the entrance of a principal singer.

Classical Period - A period roughly between the Baroque and Romantic periods, the late 18th through the early 19th centuries. Stylistically, the music of the period stresses clarity, precision, and rigid structural forms.

Coda - A trailer added on by the composer after the music's natural conclusion. The coda serves as a formal closing to the piece.

Coloratura - Literally, "colored": it refers to a soprano singing in the bel canto tradition. It is a singing technique that requires great agility, virtuosity, embellishments and ornamentation: The Queen of the Night's aria, "Zum Leiden bin ich auserkoren," from Mozart's *The Magic Flute.*

Commedia dell'arte - A popular form of dramatic presentation originating in Renaissance Italy in which highly stylized characters were involved in comic plots involving mistaken identities and misunderstandings. Two of the standard characters were Harlequin and Colombine: The "play within a play" in Leoncavallo's *I Pagliacci.*

Comprimario - A singer who performs secondary character roles such as confidantes, servants, and messengers.

Continuo, Basso continuo - A bass part (as for a keyboard or stringed instrument) that was used especially in baroque ensemble music; it consists of an independent succession of bass notes that indicate the required chords and their appropriate harmonies. Also called *figured bass, thoroughbass.*

Contralto - The lowest female voice, derived from "contra" against, and "alto" voice; a voice between the tenor and mezzo-soprano.

Countertenor - A high male voice generally singing within the female high soprano ranges.

Counterpoint - The combination of two or more independent melodies into a single harmonic texture in which each retains its linear character. The most sophisticated form of counterpoint is the fugue form, in which from two to six melodies can be used; the voices are combined, each providing a variation on the basic theme but each retaining its relation to the whole.

Crescendo - A gradual increase in the volume of a musical passage.

Da capo - Literally, "from the top"; repeat. Early 17th-century da capo arias were in the form of A B A, with the second A section repeating the first, but with ornamentation.

Deus ex machina - Literally "god out of a machine." A dramatic technique in which a person or thing appears or is introduced suddenly and unexpectedly; it provides a contrived solution to an apparently insoluble dramatic difficulty.

Diatonic - A major or minor musical scale that comprises intervals of five whole steps and two half steps.

Diminuendo - Gradually becoming softer; the opposite of crescendo.

Dissonance - A mingling of discordant sounds that do not harmonize within the diatonic scale.

Diva - Literally, "goddess"; generally the term refers to a leading female opera star who either possesses, or pretends to possess, great rank.

Dominant - The fifth tone of the diatonic scale; in the key of C, the dominant is G.

Dramatic soprano or tenor - A voice that is powerful, possesses endurance, and is generally projected in a declamatory style.

Dramma giocoso - Literally, "amusing (or humorous) drama." An opera whose story combines both serious and comic elements: Mozart's *Don Giovanni*.

Falsetto - A lighter or "false" voice; an artificially-produced high singing voice that extends above the range of the full voice.

Fioritura - It., "flowering"; a flowering ornamentation or embellishment of the vocal line within an aria.

Forte, fortissimo - Forte (*f*) means loud; mezzo forte (*mf*) is fairly loud; fortissimo (*ff*) is even louder; additional *fff*'s indicate greater degrees of loudness.

Glissando - Literally, "gliding." A rapid sliding up or down the scale.

Grand opera - An opera in which there is no spoken dialogue and the entire text is set to music, frequently treating serious and tragic subjects. Grand opera flourished in France in the 19th century (Meyerbeer); the genre is epic in scale and combines spectacle, large choruses, scenery, and huge orchestras.

Heldentenor - A tenor with a powerful dramatic voice who possesses brilliant top notes and vocal stamina. Heldentenors are well suited to heroic (Wagnerian) roles: Lauritz Melchior in Wagner's *Tristan und Isolde*.

Imbroglio - Literally, "intrigue"; an operatic scene portraying chaos and confusion, with appropriate diverse melodies and rhythms.

Largo or larghetto - Largo indicates a very slow tempo, broad and with dignity. Larghetto is at a slightly faster tempo than largo.

Legato - Literally, "tied" or "bound"; successive tones that are connected smoothly. The opposite of legato is staccato (short and plucked tones.)

Leitmotif - Literally, "leading motive." A musical fragment characterizing a person, thing, feeling, or idea that provides associations when it recurs.

Libretto - Literally, "little book"; the text of an opera.

Lied - A German song; the plural is "lieder." Originally, a German art song of the late 18th century.

Lyric - A voice that is light and delicate.

Maestro - From the Italian "master"; a term of respect to conductors, composers, directors, and great musicians.

Melodrama - Words spoken over music. Melodrama appears in Beethoven's *Fidelio* and flourished during the late 19th century in the operas of Massenet (*Manon* and *Werther*).

Mezza voce - Literally, "medium voice"; singing with medium or half volume. It is sometimes intended as a vocal means to intensify emotion.

Mezzo-soprano - A woman's voice with a range between soprano and contralto.

Obbligato - An accompaniment to a solo or principal melody that is usually played by an important, single instrument.

Octave - A musical interval embracing eight diatonic degrees; from C to C is an octave.

Opera - Literally, "work"; a dramatic or comic play in which music is the primary vehicle that conveys its story.

Opera buffa - Italian comic opera that flourished during the bel canto era. Highlighting the opera buffa genre were buffo characters who were usually basses singing patter songs: Dr. Bartolo in Rossini's *The Barber of Seville*; Dr. Dulcamara in Donizetti's *The Elixir of Love.*

Opéra comique - A French opera characterized by spoken dialogue interspersed between the musical numbers, as opposed to grand opera in which there is no spoken dialogue. Opéra comique subjects can be either comic or tragic.

Operetta, or light opera - Operas that contain comic elements and generally a light romantic plot: Strauss's *Die Fledermaus*, Offenbach's *La Périchole*, and Lehar's *The Merry Widow.* In operettas, there is usually much spoken dialogue, dancing, practical jokes, and mistaken identities.

Oratorio - A lengthy choral work, usually of a religious nature and consisting chiefly of recitatives, arias, and choruses, but performed without action or scenery: Handel's *Messiah.*

Ornamentation - Extra embellishing notes—appoggiaturas, trills, roulades, or cadenzas—that enhance a melodic line.

Overture - The orchestral introduction to a musical dramatic work that sometimes incorporates musical themes within the work. Overtures are instrumental pieces that are generally performed independently of their respective operas in concert.

Parlando - Literally, "speaking"; the imitation of speech while singing, or singing that is almost speaking over the music. Parlando sections are usually short and have minimal orchestral accompaniment.

Patter song - A song with words that are rapidly and quickly delivered. Figaro's "Largo al factotum" in Rossini's *The Barber of Seville* is a patter song.

Pentatonic - A five-note scale. Pentatonic music is most prevalent in Far Eastern countries.

Piano - A performance indication for soft volume.

Pitch - The property of a musical tone that is determined by the frequency of the waves producing it.

Pizzicato - An indication that notes are to be played by plucking the strings instead of stroking the string with the bow.

Polyphony - Literally, "many voices." A style of musical composition in which two or more independent melodies are juxtaposed; counterpoint.

Polytonal - Several tonal schemes used simultaneously.

Portamento - A continuous gliding movement from one tone to another through all the intervening pitches.

Prelude - An orchestral introduction to an act or a whole opera that precedes the opening scene.

Presto, prestissimo - Vigorous, and with the utmost speed.

Prima donna - Literally, "first lady." The female star or principal singer in an opera cast or opera company.

Prologue - A piece sung before the curtain goes up on the opera proper: Tonio's Prologue in Leoncavallo's *I Pagliacci.*

Quaver - An eighth note.

Range - The span of tonal pitch of a particular voice: soprano, mezzo-soprano, contralto, tenor, baritone, and bass.

Recitative - A formal device used to advance the plot. It is usually sung in a rhythmically free vocal style that imitates the natural inflections of speech; it conveys the dialogue and narrative in operas and oratorios. *Secco*, or dry, recitative is accompanied by harpsichord and sometimes with other continuo instruments; *accompagnato* indicates that the recitative is accompanied by the orchestra.

Ritornello - A refrain, or short recurrent instrumental passage between elements of a vocal composition.

Romanza - A solo song that is usually sentimental; it is shorter and less complex than an aria and rarely deals with terror, rage, or anger.

Romantic Period - The Romantic period is usually considered to be between the early 19th and early 20th centuries. Romanticists found inspiration in nature and man. Von Weber's *Der Freischütz* and Beethoven's *Fidelio* (1805) are considered the first German Romantic operas; many of Verdi's operas as well as the early operas of Wagner are also considered Romantic operas.

Roulade - A florid, embellished melody sung to one syllable.

Rubato - An expressive technique, literally meaning "robbed"; it is a fluctuation of tempo within a musical phrase, often against a rhythmically steady accompaniment.

Secco - "Dry"; the type of accompaniment for recitative played by the harpsichord and sometimes continuo instruments.

Semitone - A half step, the smallest distance between two notes. In the key of C, the half steps are from E to F and from B to C.

Serial music - Music based on a series of tones in a chosen pattern without regard for traditional tonality.

Sforzando - Sudden loudness and force; it must stand out from the texture and be emphasized by an accent.

Singspiel - Literally, "song drama." Early German style of opera employing spoken dialogue between songs: Mozart's *The Magic Flute.*

Soprano - The highest range of the female voice ranging from lyric (light and graceful quality) to dramatic (fuller and heavier in tone).

Sotto voce - Literally, "below the voice"; sung softly between a whisper and a quiet conversational tone.

Soubrette - A soprano who sings supporting roles in comic opera: Adele in Strauss's *Die Fledermaus*; Despina in Mozart's *Così fan tutte.*

Spinto - From the Italian "spingere" (to push); a singer with lyric vocal qualities who "pushes" the voice to achieve heavier dramatic qualities.

Sprechstimme - Literally, "speaking voice." The singer half sings a note and half speaks; the declamation sounds like speaking but the duration of pitch makes it seem almost like singing.

Staccato - Short, clipped, detached, rapid articulation; the opposite of legato.

Stretto - Literally, "narrow." A concluding passage performed in a quick tempo to create a musical climax.

Strophe - Strophe is a rhythmic system of repeating lines. A musical setting of a strophic text is characterized by the repetition of the same music for all strophes.

Syncopation - A shifting of the beat forward or back from its usual place in the bar; a temporary displacement of the regular metrical accent in music caused typically by stressing the weak beat.

Supernumerary - A "super"; a performer with a non-singing and non-speaking role: "Spear-carrier."

Symphonic poem - A large orchestral work in one continuous movement, usually narrative or descriptive in character: Franz Liszt's *Les Preludes*; Richard Strauss's *Don Juan, Till Eulenspiegel,* and *Ein Heldenleben.*

Tempo - The speed at which music is performed.

Tenor - The highest natural male voice.

Tessitura - The usual range of a voice part.

Tonality - The organization of all the tones and harmonies of a piece of music in relation to a tonic (the first tone of its scale).

Tone poem - An orchestral piece with a program.

Tonic - The principal tone of the key in which a piece is written. C is the tonic of C major.

Trill - Two adjacent notes rapidly and repeatedly alternated.

Tutti - All together.

Twelve-tone - The twelve chromatic tones of the octave placed in a chosen fixed order and constituting, with some permitted permutations and derivations, the melodic and harmonic material of a serial musical piece. Each note of the chromatic scale is used as part of the melody before any other note is repeated.

Verismo - Literally "truth"; the artistic use of contemporary everyday material in preference to the heroic or legendary in opera. A movement particularly in Italian opera during the late 19th and early 20th centuries: Mascagni's *Cavalleria rusticana*.

Vibrato - A "vibration"; a slightly tremulous effect imparted to vocal or instrumental tone to enrich and intensify sound, and add warmth and expressiveness through slight and rapid variations in pitch.

Opera Journeys™ Mini Guide Series

Opera Journeys™ Libretto Series

Opera Classics Library™ Series

A History of Opera: Milestones and Metamorphoses

Puccini Companion: the Glorious Dozen

Mozart's da Ponte Operas

Fifty Timeless Opera Classics

PUCCINI COMPANION: THE GLORIOUS DOZEN

756-page Soft Cover volume

Each Puccini Chapter features:

COMPLETE LIBRETTO
Italian-English side-by-side

STORY NARRATIVE
with 100s of Music Highlight Examples

ANALYSIS AND COMMENTARY

Print or Ebook

A HISTORY of OPERA: MILESTONES and METAMORPHOSES

432 pages, soft cover / 21 chapters

featuring   **0ver 250 music examples**

• A comprehensive survey of milestones in opera history
• All periods are analyzed in depth:
Baroque, Classical, Romantic, Bel Canto, Opera Buffa, German Romanticism, Wagner and music drama, Verismo,
plus analyses of the "Tristan Chord," atonalism, minimalism...

Print or Ebook

OPERA JOURNEYS' COLLECTION: FIFTY TIMELESS OPERA CLASSICS

816-page Soft Cover volume

Print or EBook

*A collection of fifty·of the most popular operas
in the Opera Journeys Mini Guide Series,
each with Story Narrative and 100s of Music Examples,
PLUS insightful,in delpth commentary and analysis*

MOZART'S DA PONTE OPERAS:

Don Giovanni, The Marriage of Figaro, Così fan tutte

348-page Soft or Hard Cover Edition

Print or Ebook

**Mozart: Master of Musical Characterization;
Da Ponte: Ambassador of Italian Culture.**

Featuring: Principal Characters, Brief Story Synopsis, Story Narrative, Music Highlight Examples, and insightful in depth Commentary and Analysis, PLUS a newly translated LIBRETTO of each opera with Italian/English translation side-by-side.

ORDER: Opera Journeys' Web Site www.operajourneys.com

OPERA JOURNEYS LIBRETTO SERIES
Print or Ebook

New translations (side-by-side) with Music Highlight Examples

•Aida　•The Barber of Seville　•La Bohème
•Carmen　•Cavalleria Rusticana　•La Cenerentola
•Così fan tutte　•Don Carlo　•Don Giovanni
•La Fanciulla del West　•Gianni Schicchi
•Lucia di Lammermoor　•Madama Butterfly
•The Magic Flute　•Manon Lescaut
•The Marriage of Figaro　•A Masked Ball
•Otello　•I Pagliacci　•Rigoletto　•La Rondine
•Salome　Samson and Delilah　•Suor Angelica
•Il Tabarro •Tosca　•La Traviata　•Il Trovatore　•Turandot

OPERA JOURNEYS MINI GUIDE SERIES
Print or Ebook

featuring 125 titles

• *Brief Story Synopsis*

• *Principal Characters*

• *Story Narrative*

• *Music Highlight Examples*

• *Commentary and Analysis*

•The Abduction from the Seraglio •Adriana Lecouvreur •L'Africaine •Aida •Andrea Chénier
•Anna Bolena •Ariadne auf Naxos •Armida •Attila •The Ballad of Baby Doe •The Barber of Seville
•Duke Bluebeard's Castle •La Bohème •Boris Godunov •Candide •Capriccio •Carmen
•Cavalleria Rusticana •Cendrillon •La Cenerentola •La Clemenza di Tito •Le Comte Ory
•Così fan tutte •The Crucible •La Damnation de Faust •The Death of Klinghoffer •Doctor Atomic
• Don Carlo • Don Giovanni •Don Pasquale •La Donna del Lago •The Elixir of Love •Elektra
•Ernani •Eugene Onegin •Exploring Wagner's Ring •Falstaff •La Fanciulla del West •Faust
•La Fille du Régiment •Fidelio •Die Fledermaus •The Flying Dutchman •Die Frau ohne Schatten
•Der Freischütz •Gianni Schicchi •La Gioconda •Hamlet •Hansel and Gretel •Henry VIII
•Iolanta •L'Italiana in Algeri •Les Huguenots •Iphigénie en Tauride •Julius Caesar •Lakmé
•Lohengrin •Lucia di Lammermoor •Macbeth •Madama Butterfly •The Magic Flute
•The Makropolis Case •Manon •Manon Lescaut •Maria Stuarda •The Marriage of Figaro
•A Masked Ball •Die Meistersinger •The Mikado •Nabucco •Nixon in China •Norma
•Of Mice and Men •Orfeo ed Euridice •Otello •I Pagliacci •Parsifal •The Pearl Fishers
•Pelléas et Mélisande •Porgy and Bess •Prince Igor •I Puritani •The Queen of Spades
•The Rake's Progress •The Rape of Lucretia •The Rhinegold •Rigoletto •The Ring of the Nibelung
•Roberto Devereaux •Rodalinda •Roméo et Juliette •La Rondine •Der Rosenkavalier •Rusalka
•Salome •Samson and Delilah •Show Boat •Siegfried •Simon Boccanegra •La Sonnambula
•Suor Angelica •Susannah •Il Tabarro •The Tales of Hoffmann •Tannhäuser •Thaïs •Tosca
•La Traviata •Tristan and Isolde •Il Trittico •Les Troyens •Il Trovatore •Turandot
•Twilight of the Gods •The Valkyrie •Werther •West Side Story •Wozzeck

ORDER: Opera Journeys' Web Site www.operajourneys.com

Made in the USA
Middletown, DE
30 July 2018